Compositions Book 5

Music
for Chorus:
Smaller Works

by
Ken Langer

Compositions Book 5

Original Music for Chorus: Smaller Works

by
Ken Langer

Compositions Book 5
Music for Chorus: Smaller Works
by Ken Langer

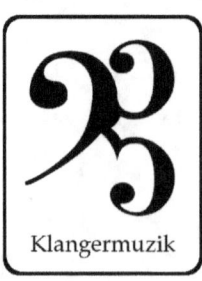

Klangermuzik

Klangermuzik
http://www.klangermuzik.com

First Edition (Softcover)

Copyright © 2013, Ken Langer

ISBN: 978-1-300-74395-8

Produced in the United States of America

The author may be contacted at ken@kenlanger.com.

Table of Contents

Introduction

This book is a collection of original compositions for chorus. The works in this collection are generally shorter in length than the works included in my Book Three and include work for smaller size choirs. These shorter works include rounds, canons, and hymns.

Recordings of all the works can be found on my website: http://kenlanger.com. Some of the recordings are live while others are MIDI transcriptions which may help you become familiar with each work.

Dancing In Circles

Ken Langer

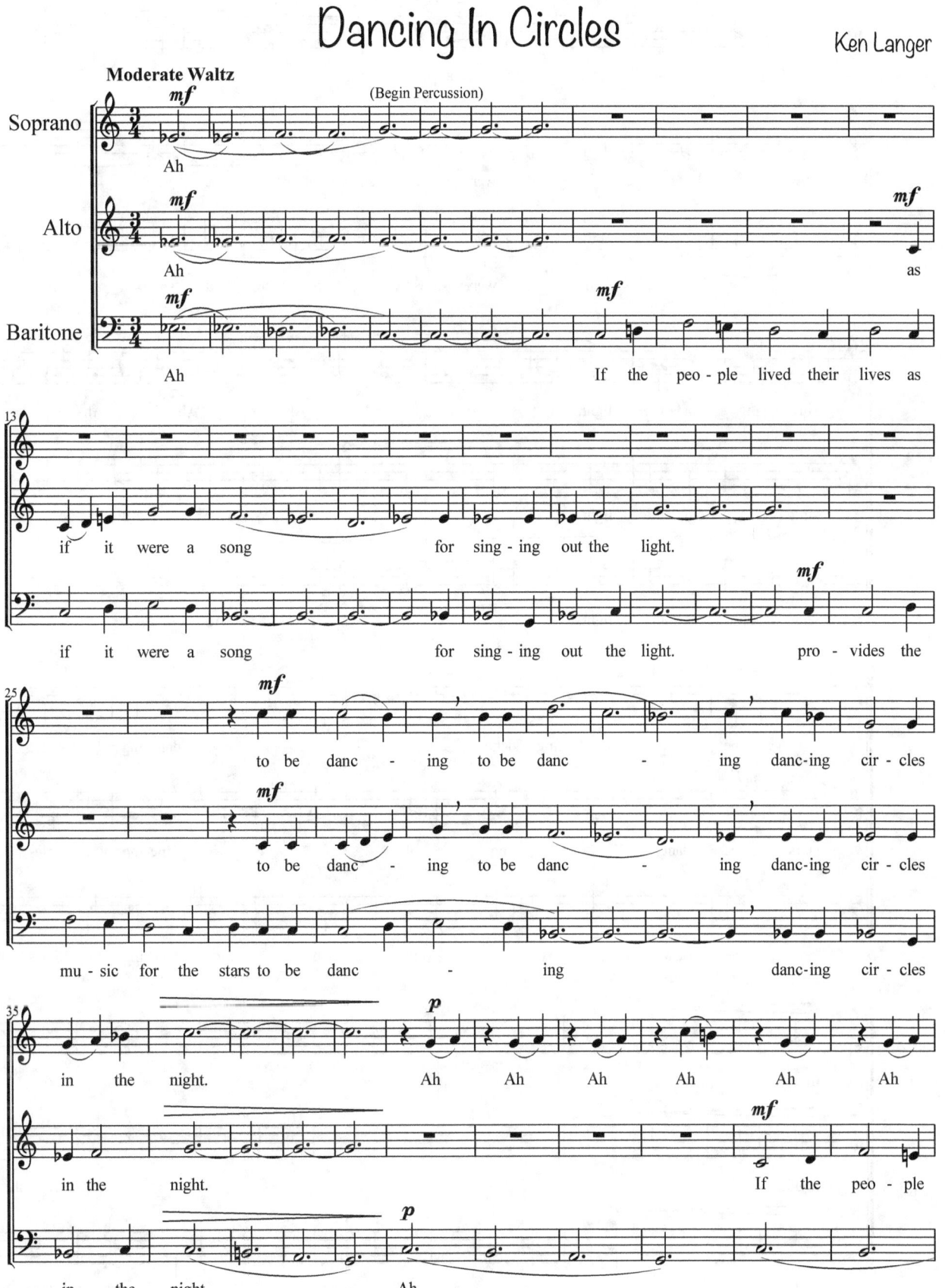

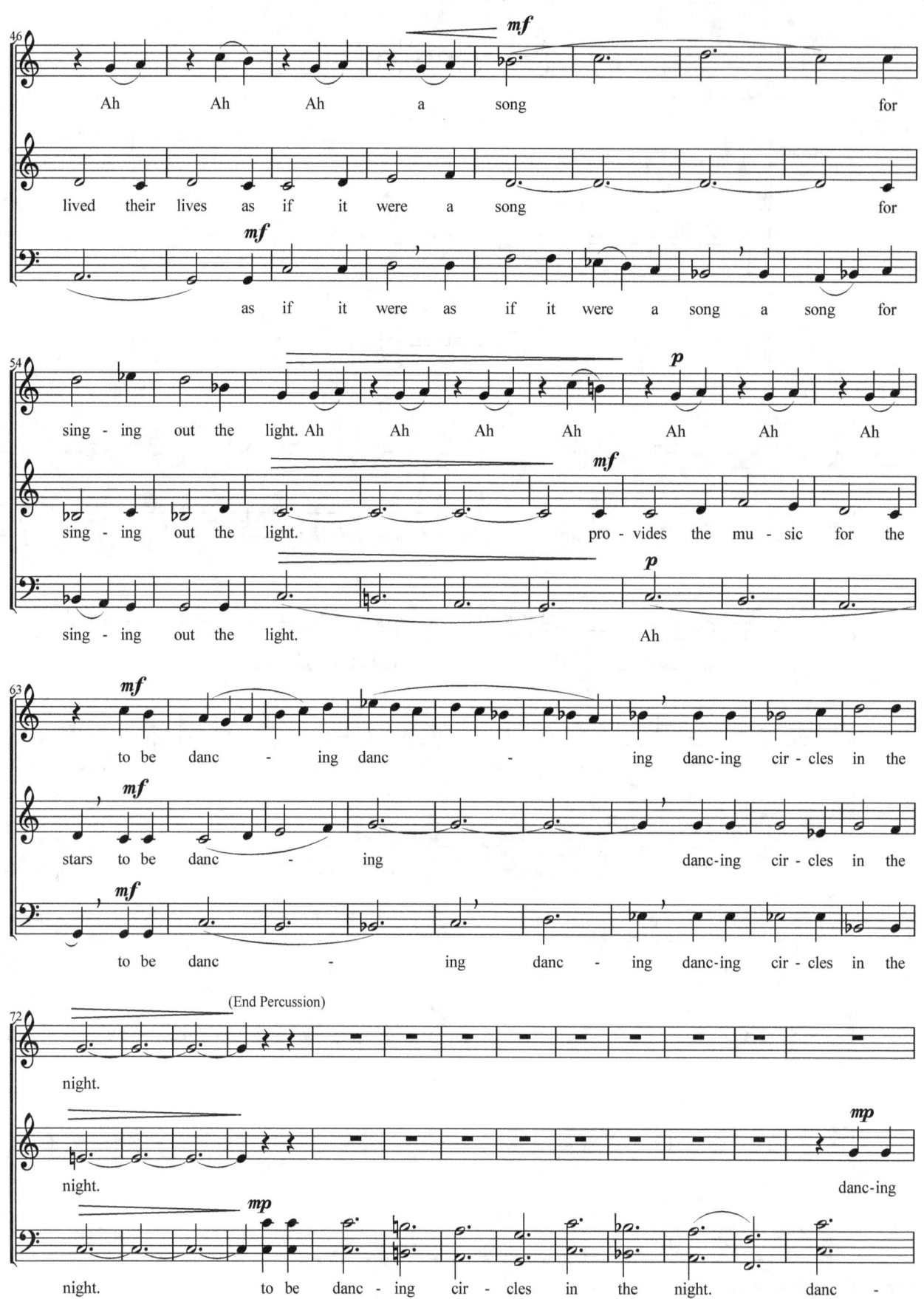

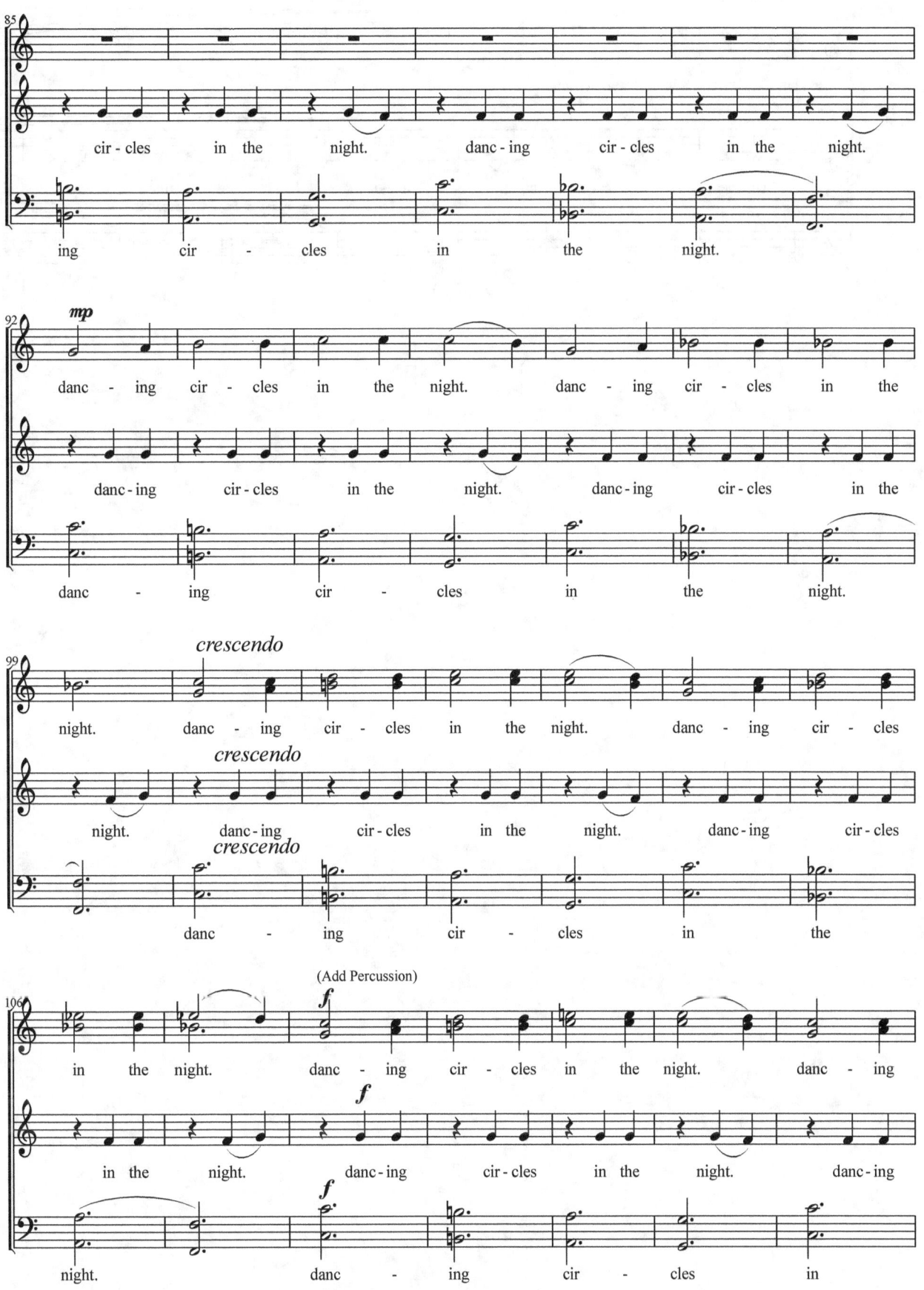

11

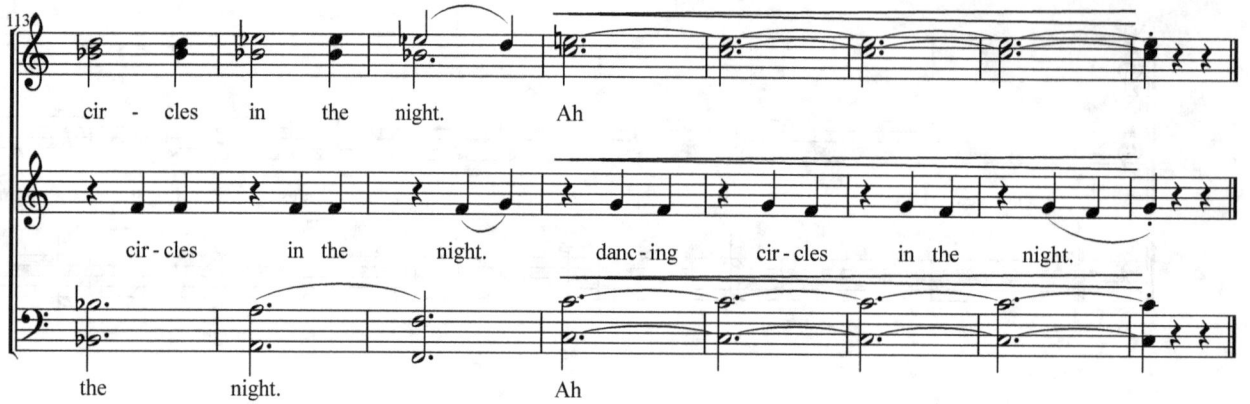

cir - cles   in   the   night.   Ah

cir - cles   in   the   night.   danc - ing   cir - cles   in   the   night.

the   night.   Ah

Day Is Done

Ken Langer

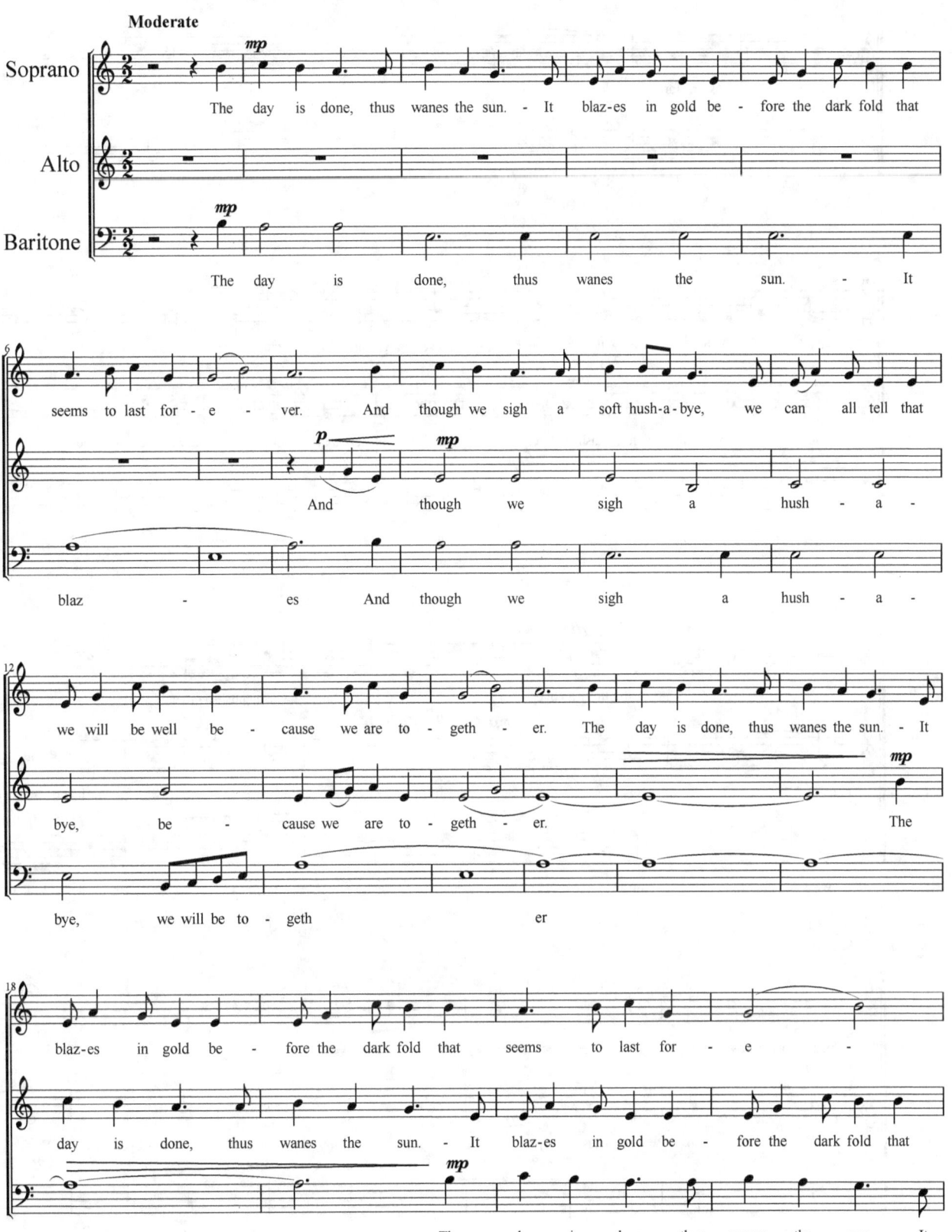

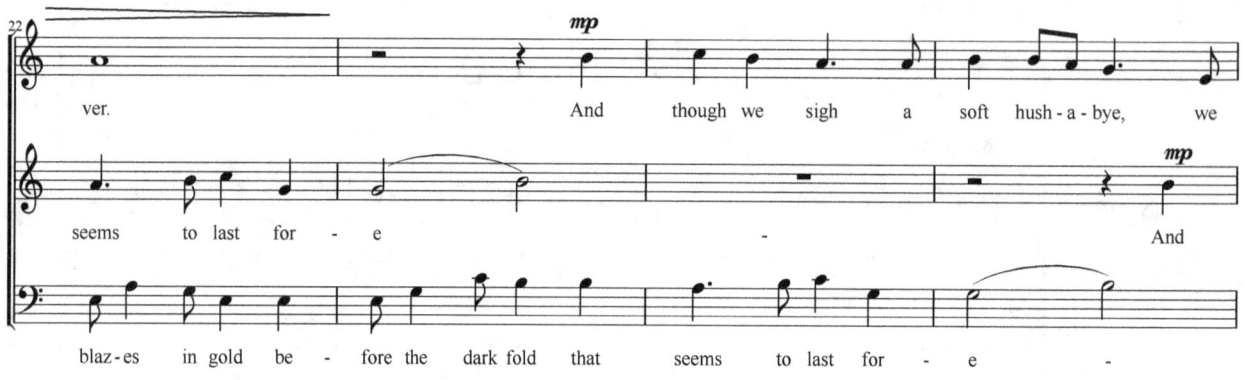

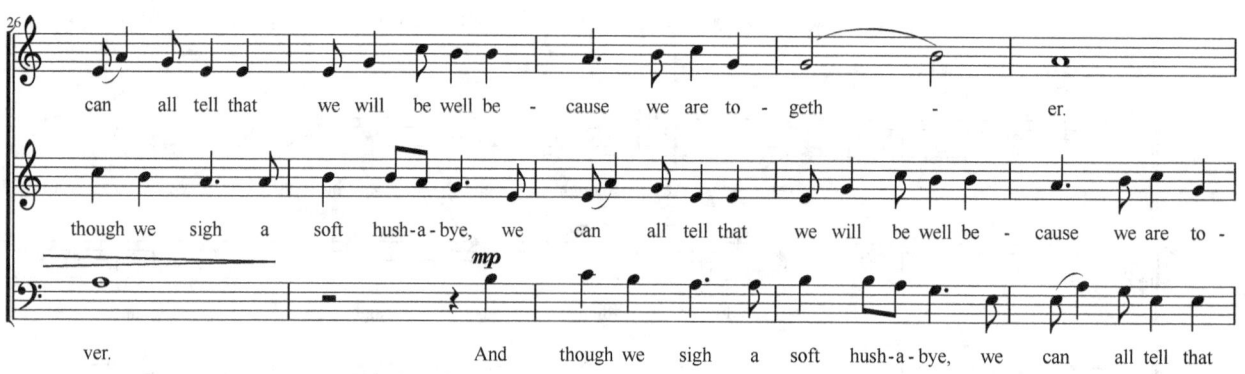

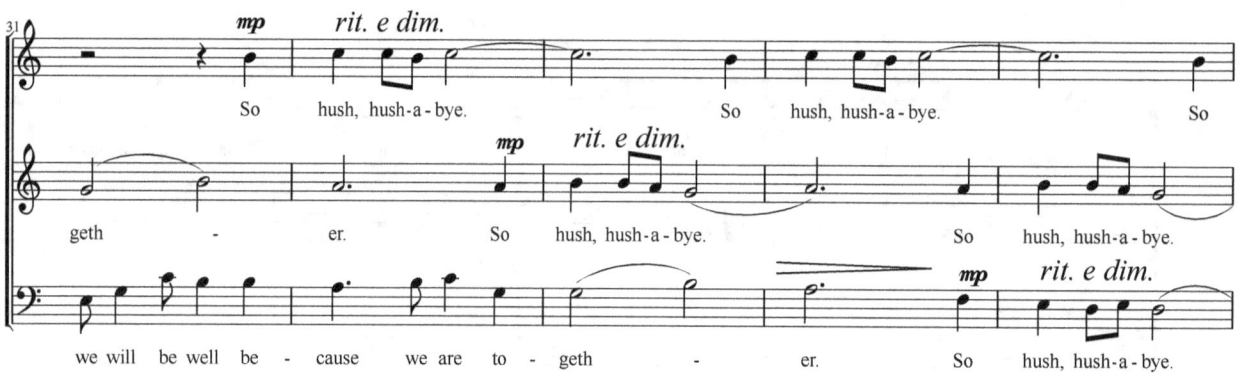

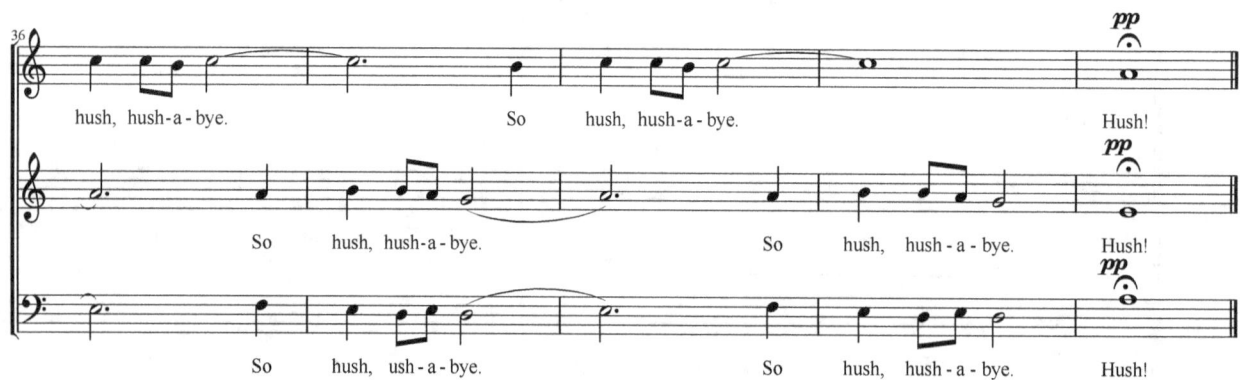

Text adopted from the Tao Te Ching

The Eternal Tao

Ken Langer

note: any text may be adapted to this chant formula

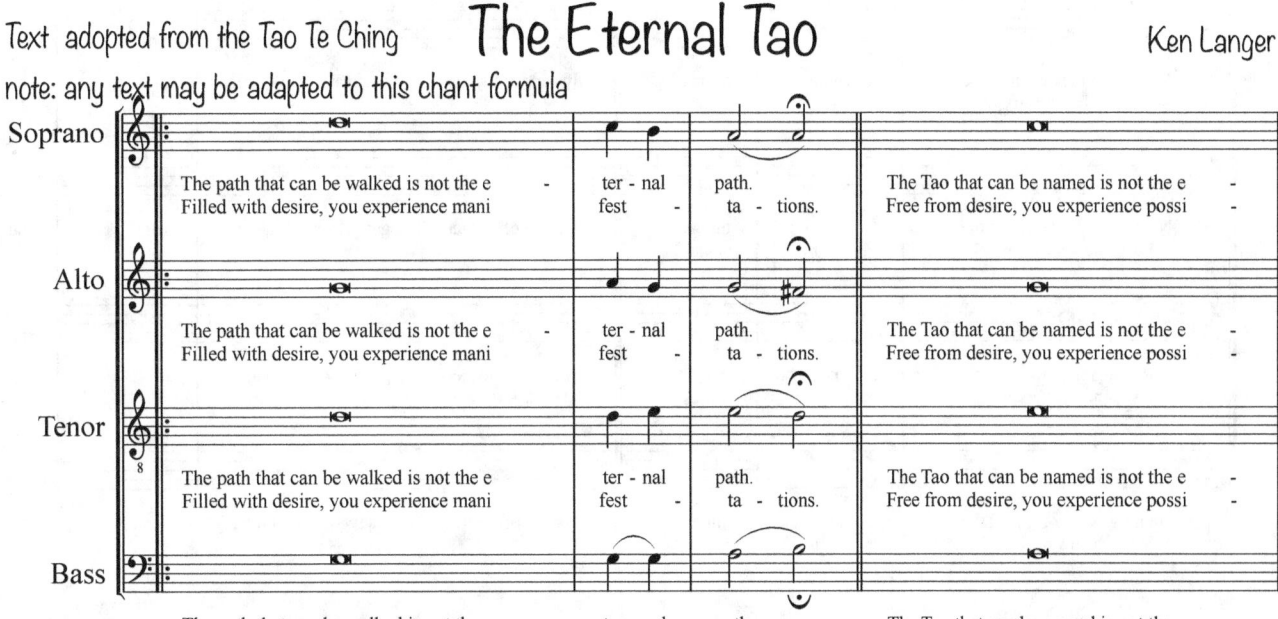

The path that can be walked is not the e - ter - nal path.
Filled with desire, you experience mani - fest - ta - tions.
The Tao that can be named is not the e -

Free from desire, you experience possi -

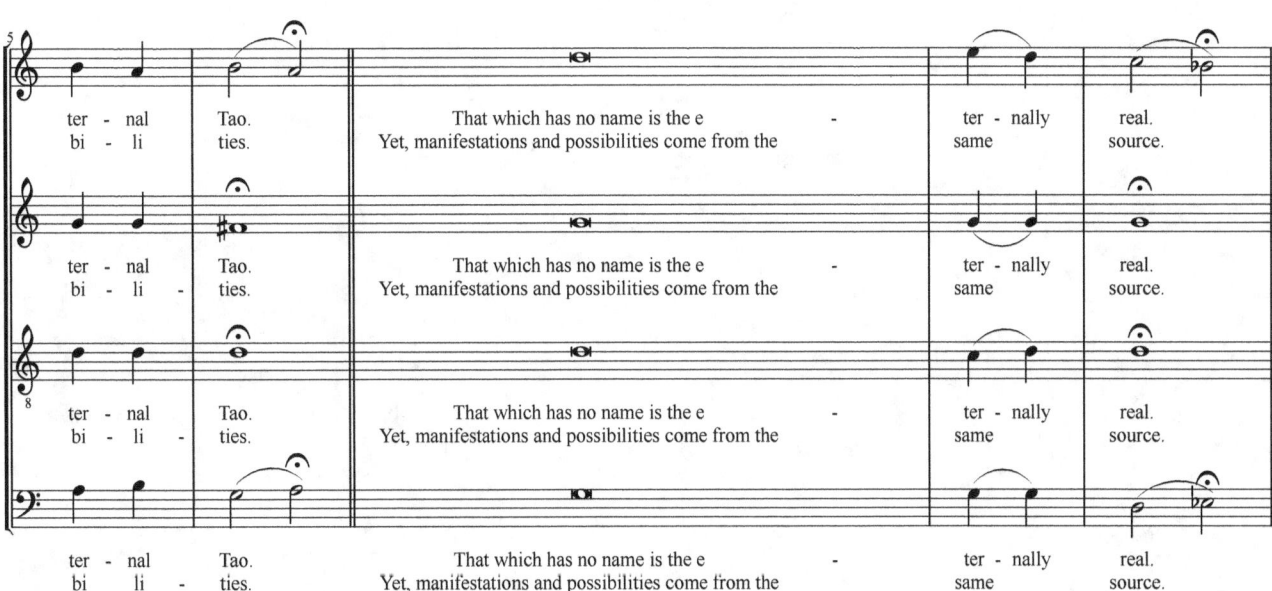

ter - nal Tao. That which has no name is the e - ter - nally real.
bi - li - ties. Yet, manifestations and possibilities come from the same source.

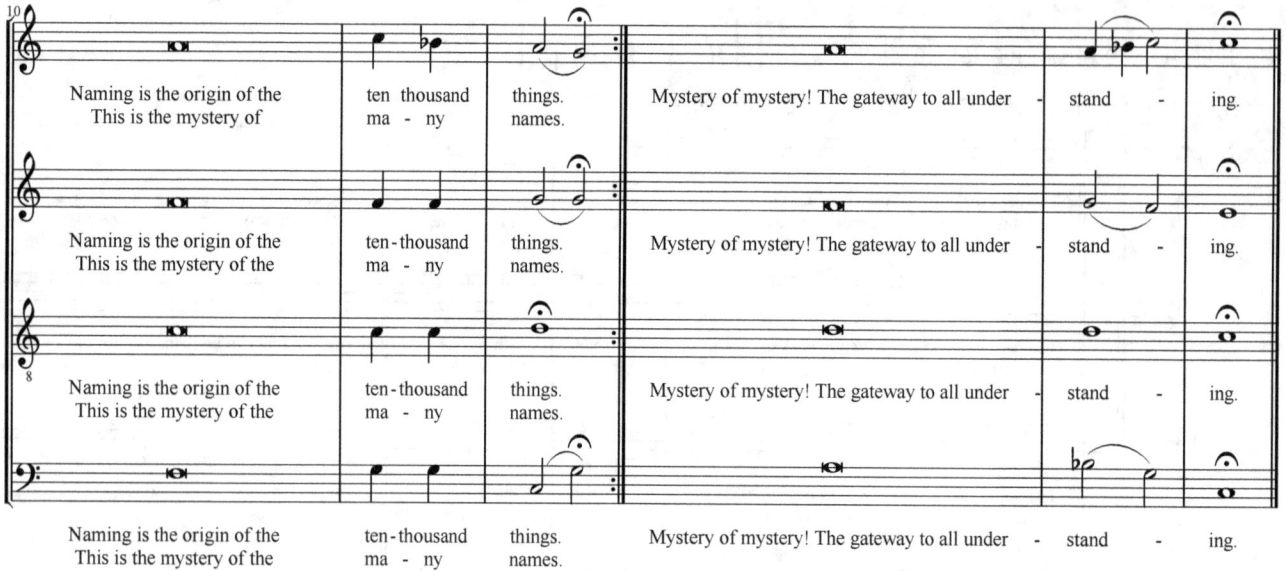

Naming is the origin of the ten thousand things.
This is the mystery of the ma - ny names.

Mystery of mystery! The gateway to all under - stand - ing.

the text may be changed
to suit the occasion

Hey Yah

Ken Langer

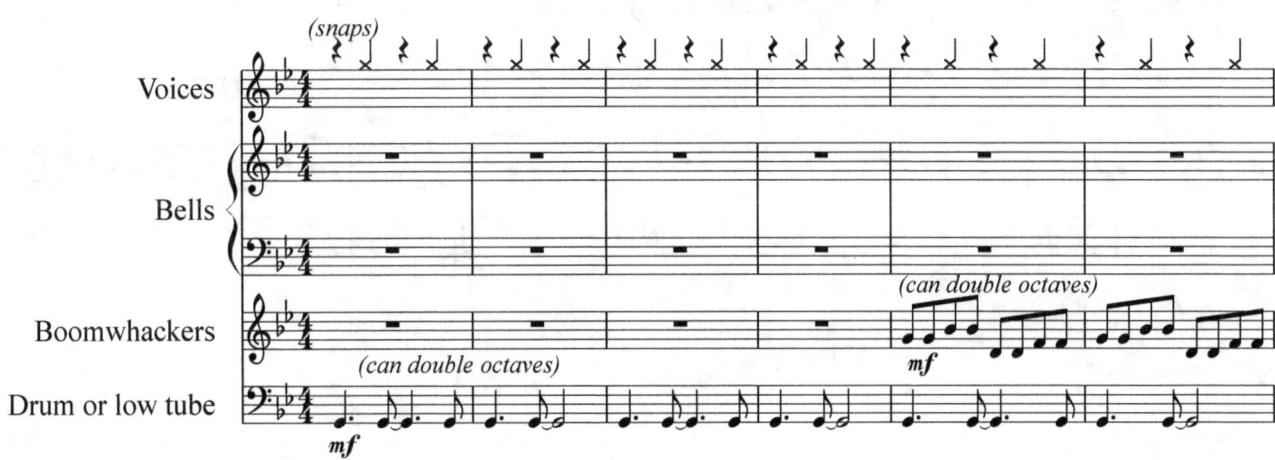

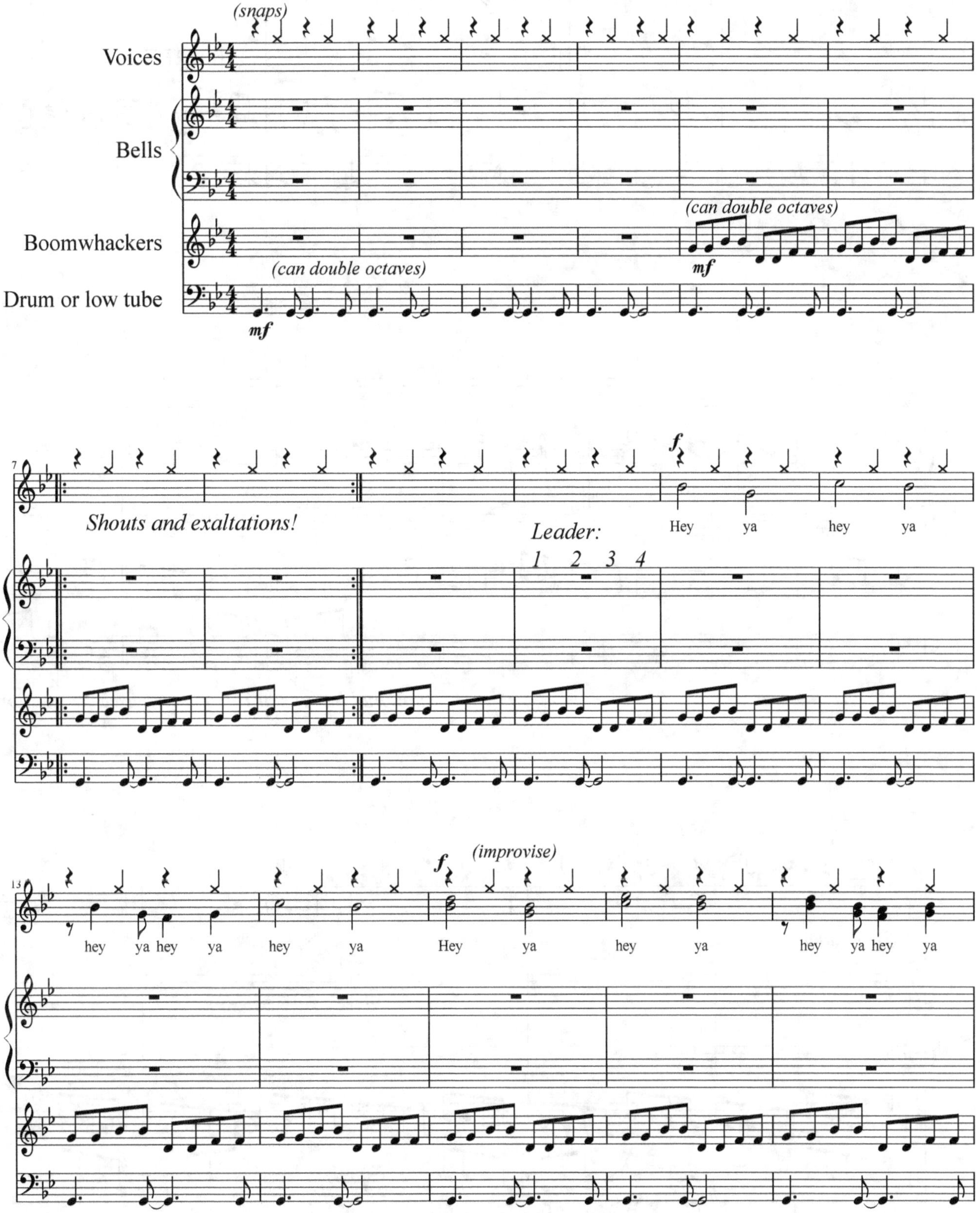

Shouts and exaltations!

Leader:
1 2 3 4

Hey ya hey ya

hey ya hey ya hey ya Hey ya hey ya hey ya hey ya

(improvise)

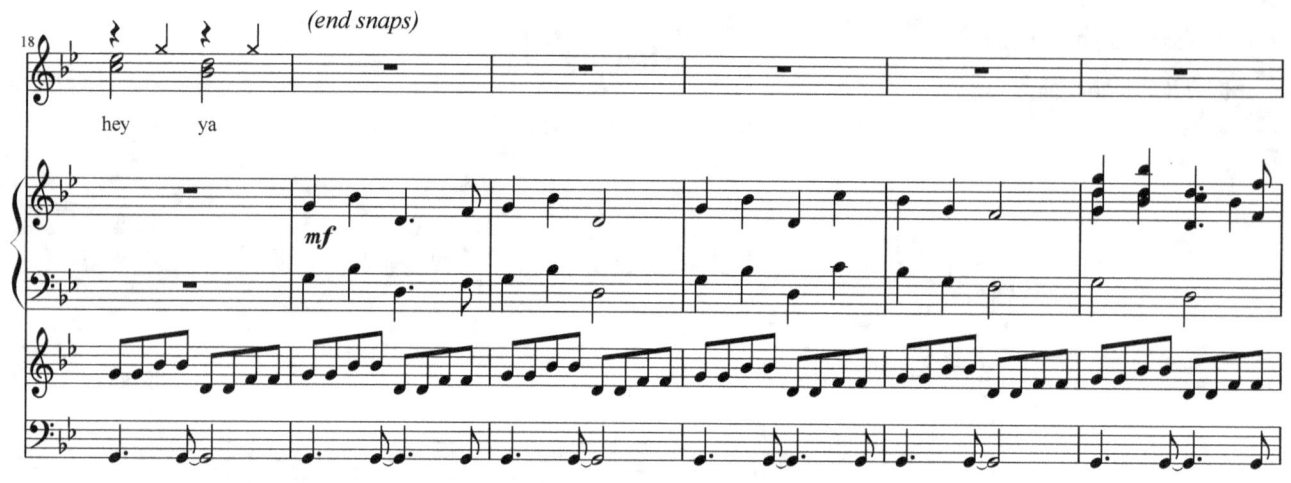

(end snaps)

hey ya

mf

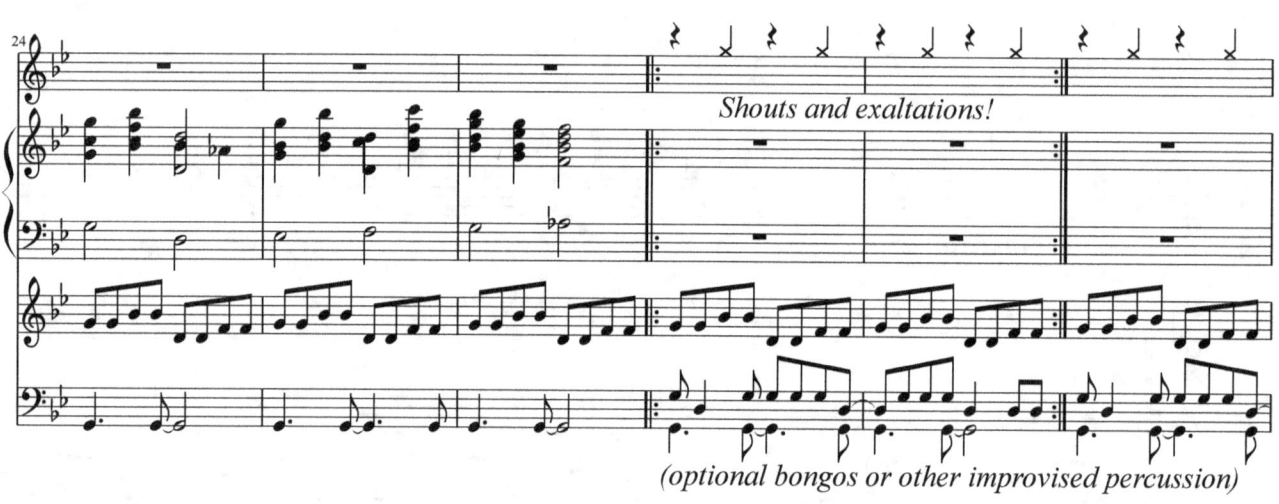

Shouts and exaltations!

(optional bongos or other improvised percussion)

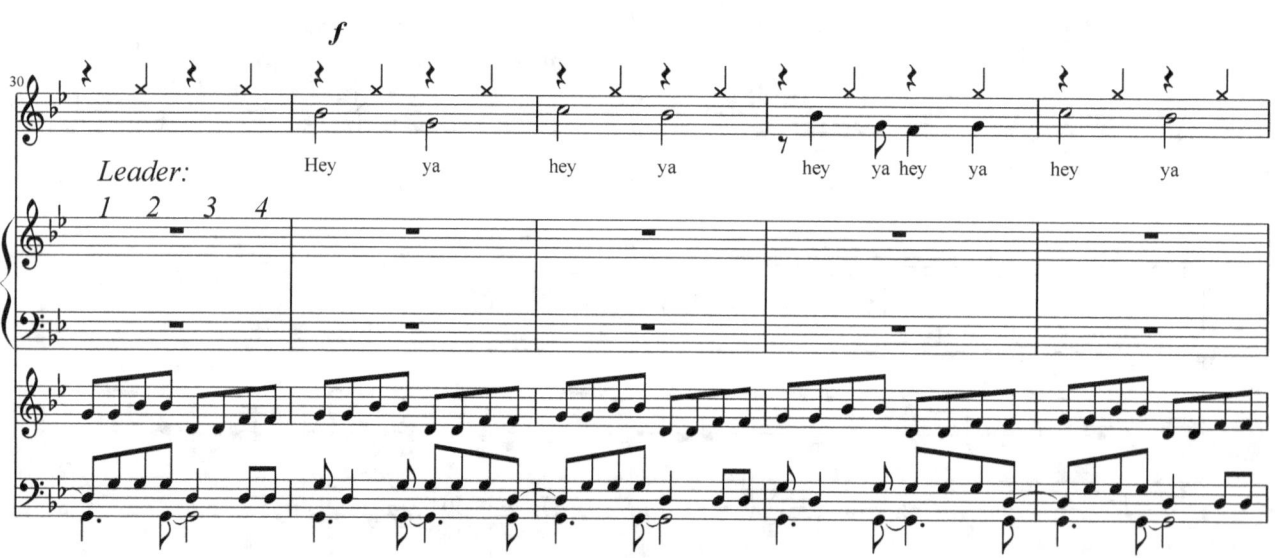

f

Leader:
1 2 3 4

Hey ya hey ya hey ya hey ya hey ya

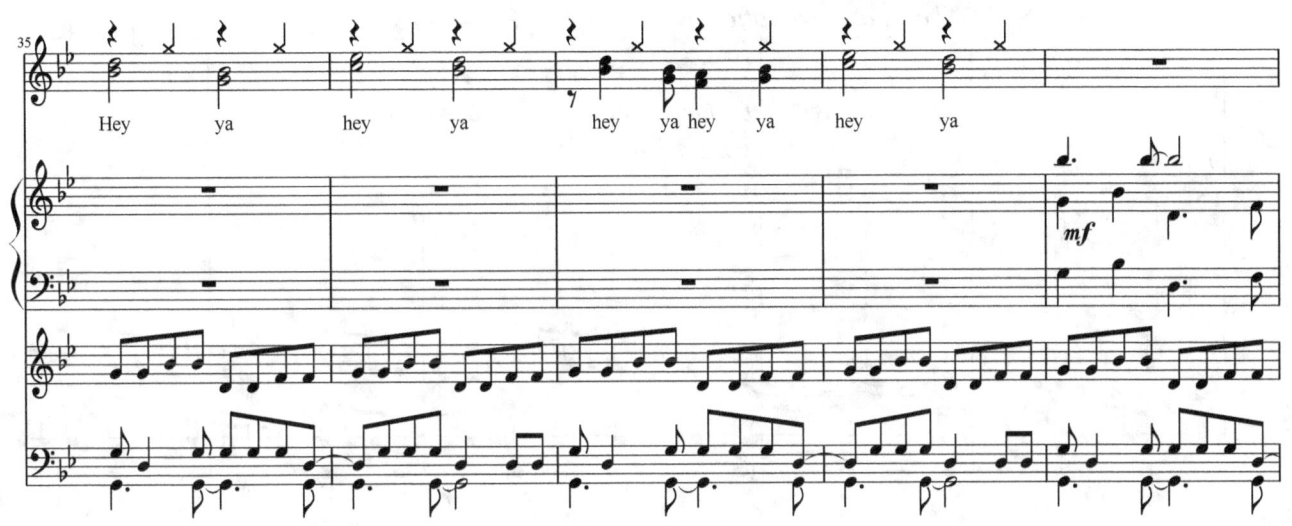

Hey   ya   hey   ya   hey   ya hey   ya   hey   ya

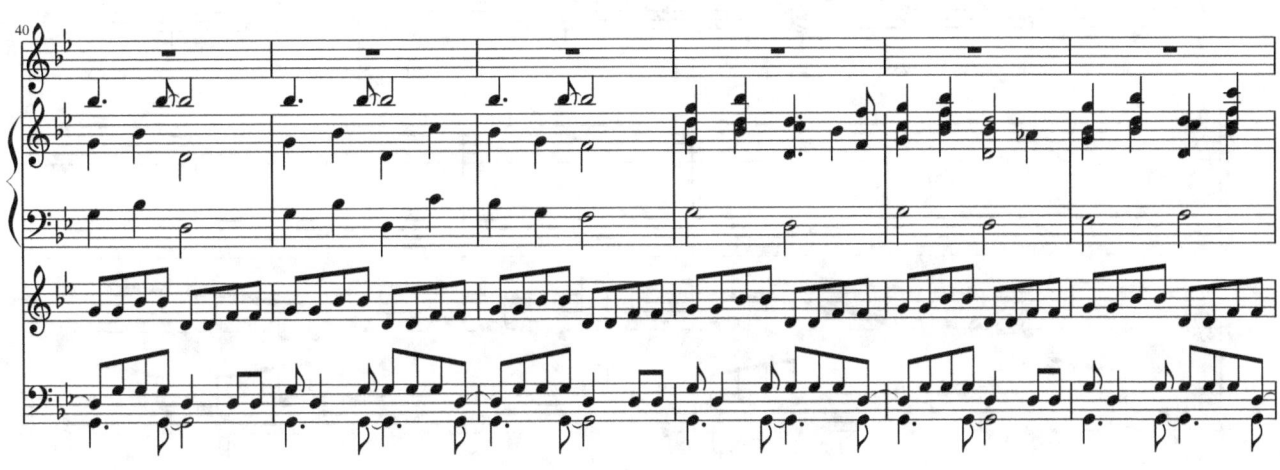

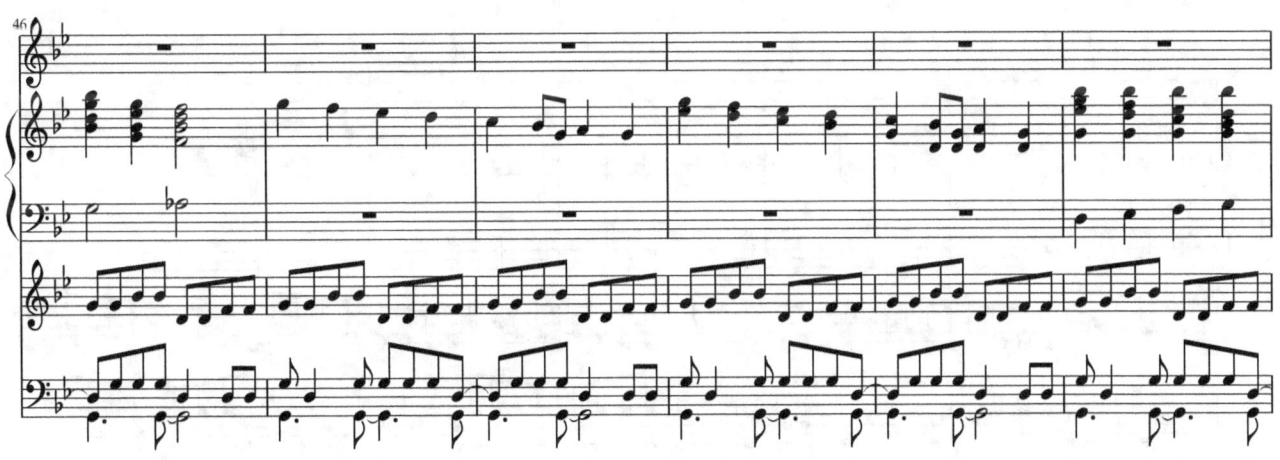

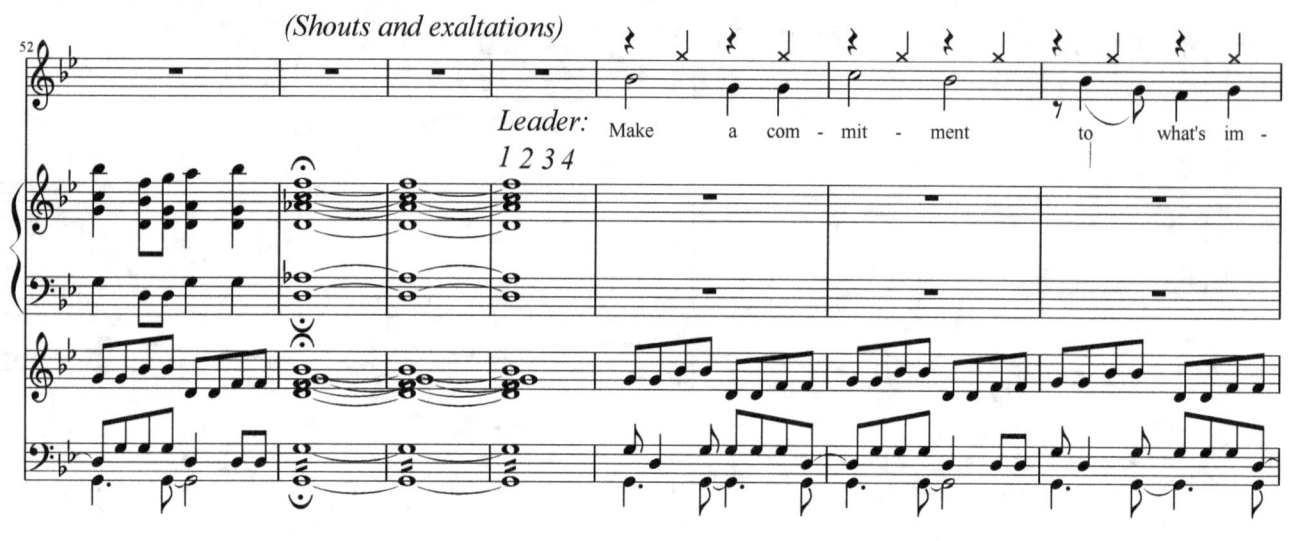

(Shouts and exaltations)

Leader: Make a com - mit - ment to what's im -
1 2 3 4

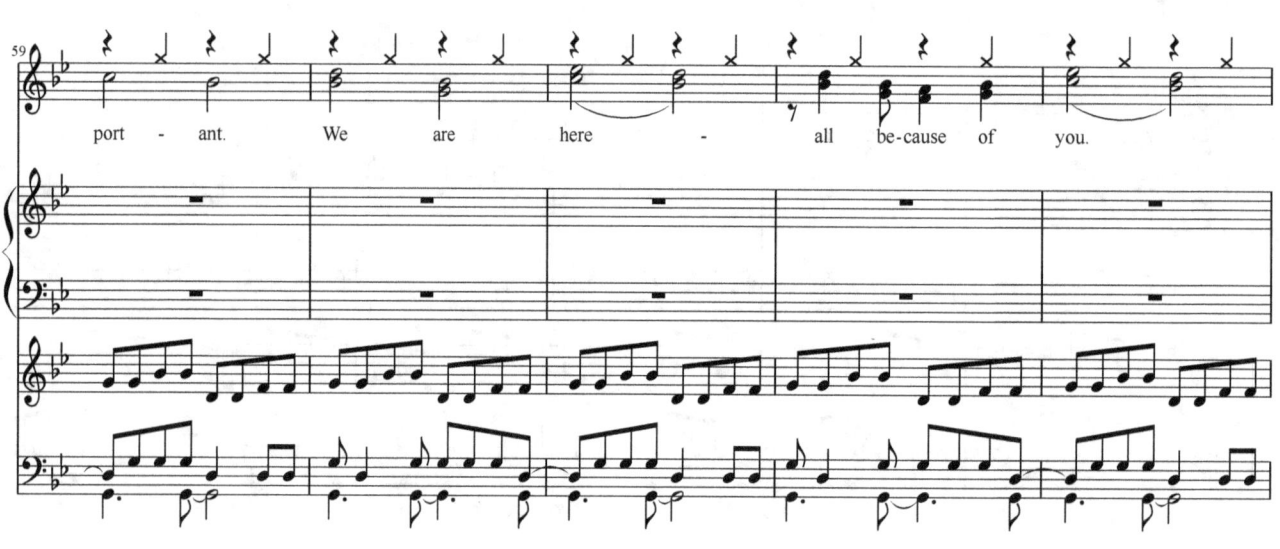

port - ant. We are here - all be-cause of you.

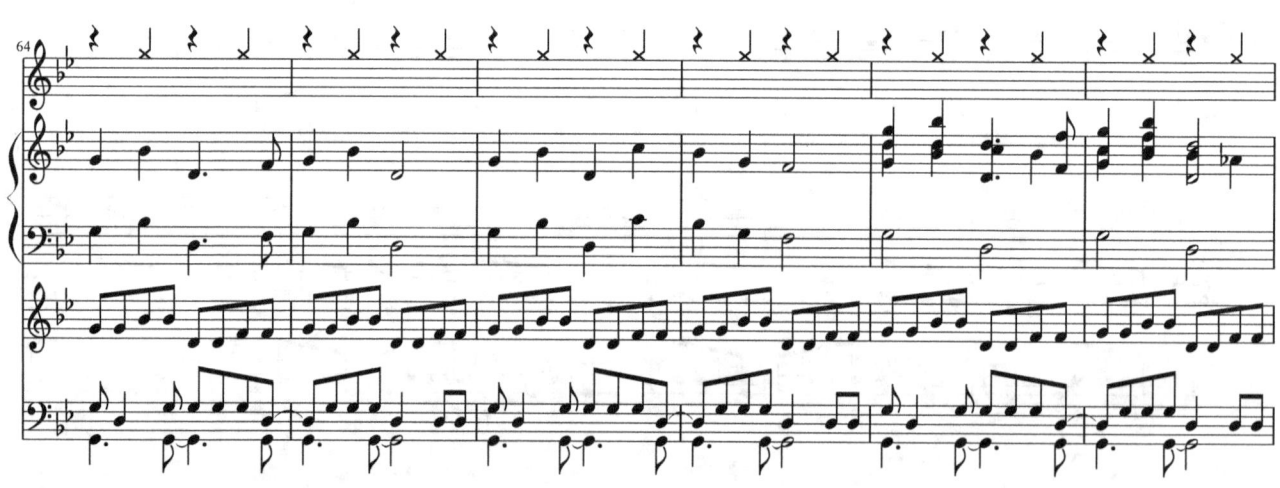

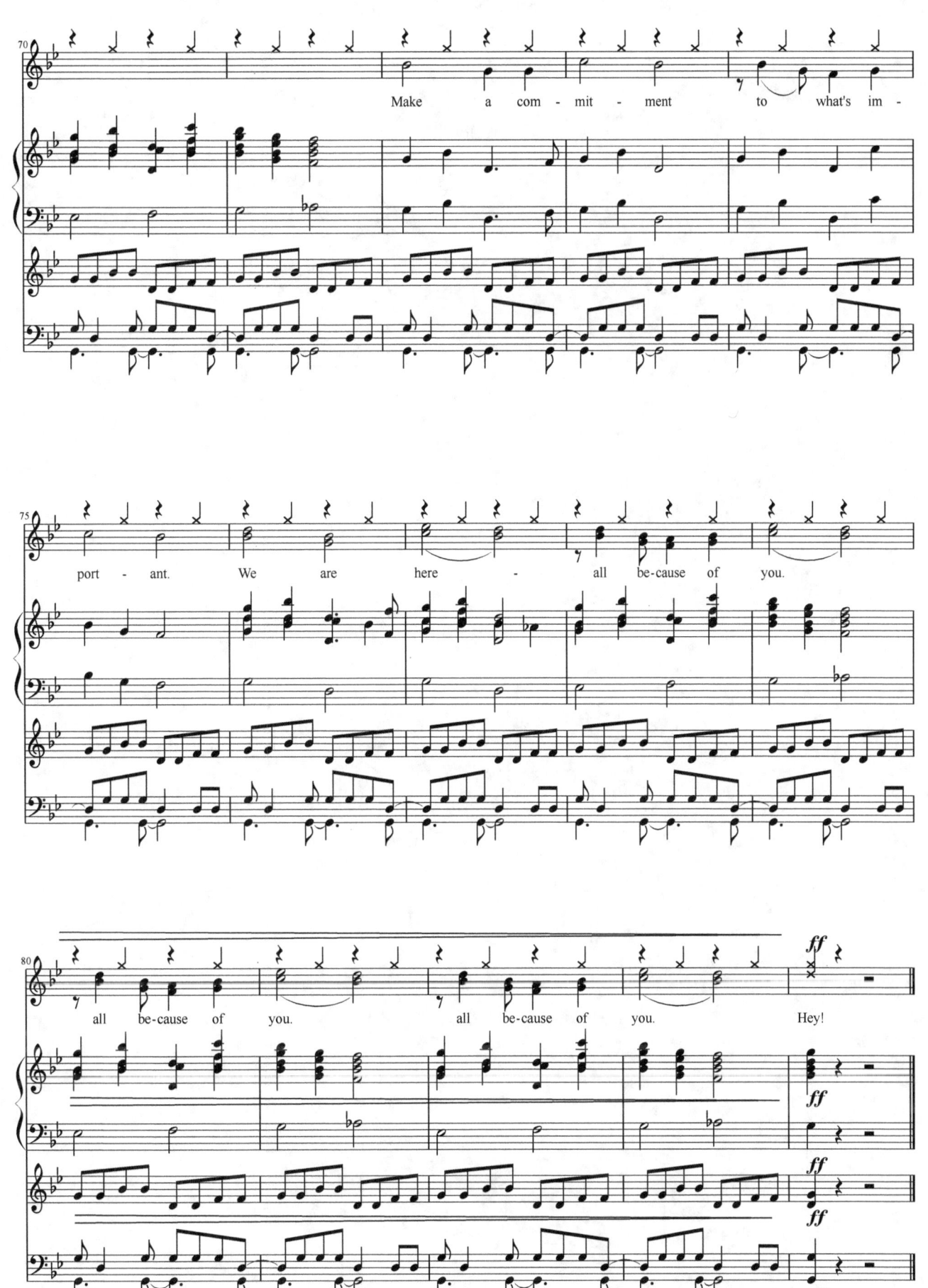

Make a com - mit - ment to what's im -

port - ant. We are here - all be-cause of you.

all be-cause of you. all be-cause of you. Hey!

Mother Earth

Ken Langer

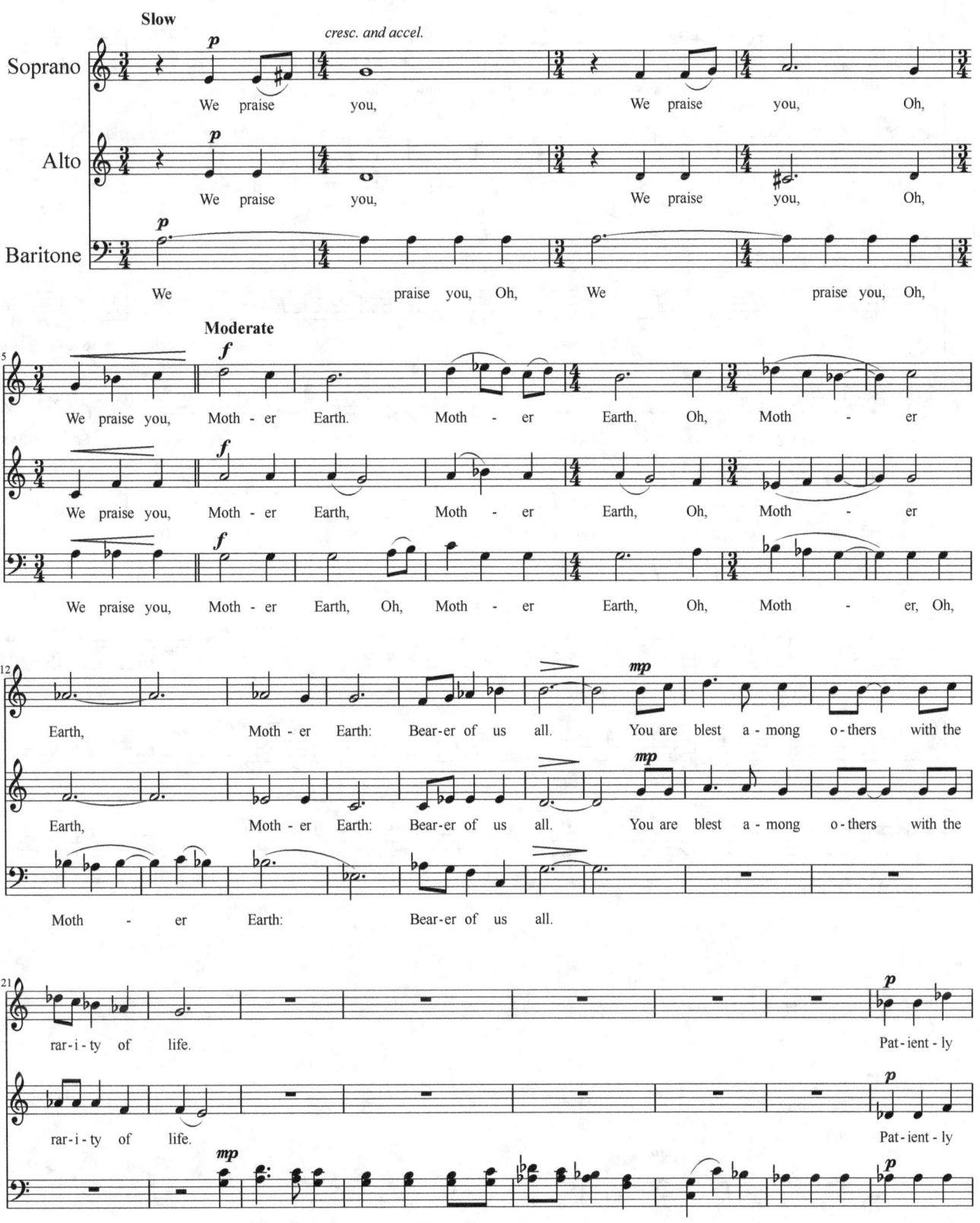

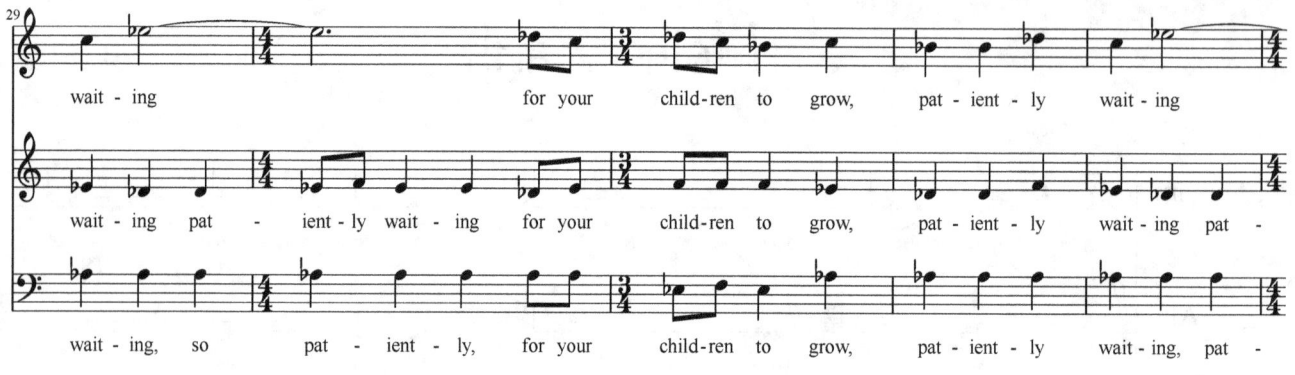

wait - ing for your child-ren to grow, pat - ient - ly wait - ing

wait - ing pat - ient - ly wait - ing for your child-ren to grow, pat - i - ent - ly wait - ing pat -

wait - ing, so pat - i - ent - ly, for your child-ren to grow, pat - i - ent - ly wait - ing, pat -

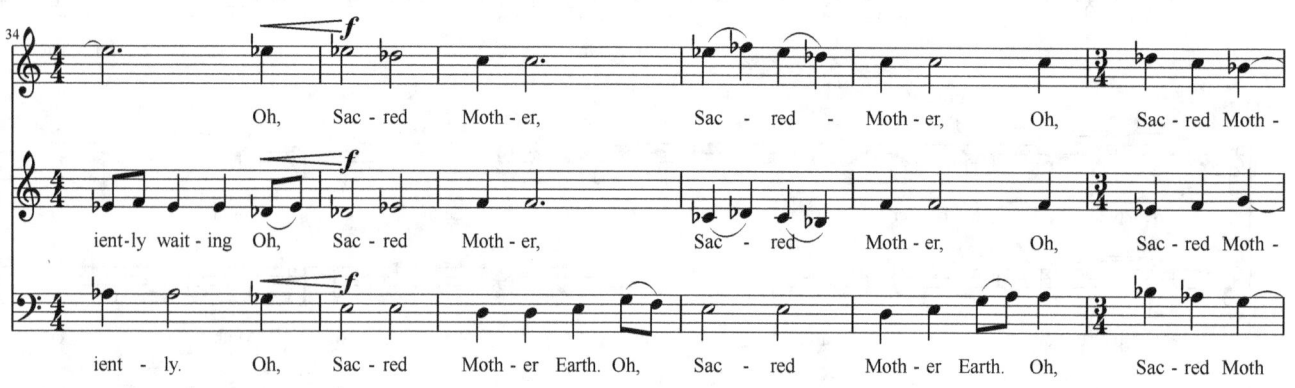

Oh, Sac - red Moth - er, Sac - red - Moth - er, Oh, Sac - red Moth -

ient-ly wait - ing Oh, Sac - red Moth - er, Sac - red Moth - er, Oh, Sac - red Moth -

ient - ly. Oh, Sac - red Moth - er Earth. Oh, Sac - red Moth - er Earth. Oh, Sac - red Moth

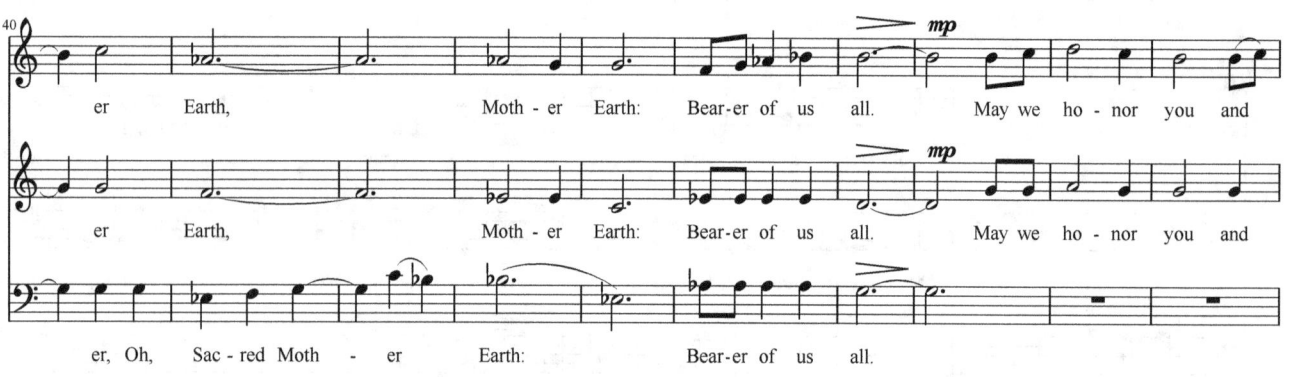

er Earth, Moth - er Earth: Bear-er of us all. May we ho - nor you and

er Earth, Moth - er Earth: Bear-er of us all. May we ho - nor you and

er, Oh, Sac - red Moth - er Earth: Bear-er of us all.

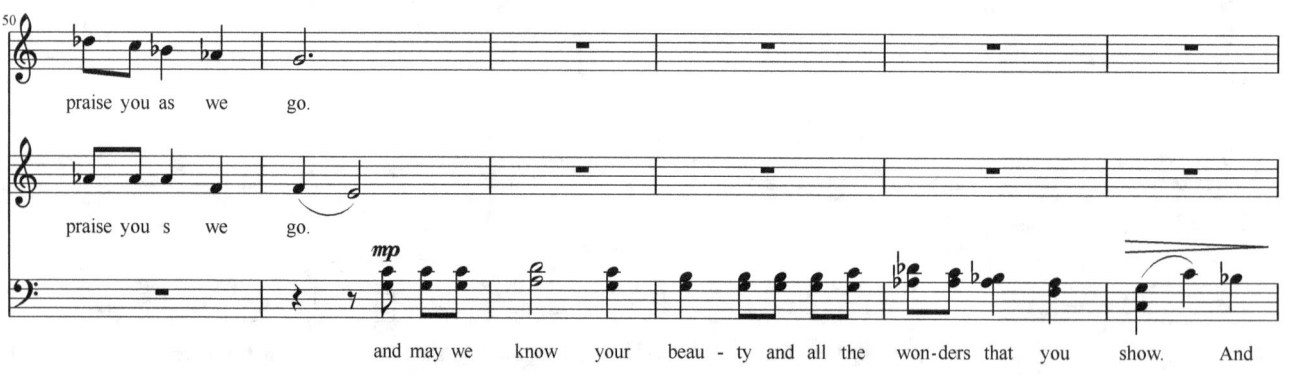

praise you as we go.

praise you s we go.

and may we know your beau - ty and all the won-ders that you show. And

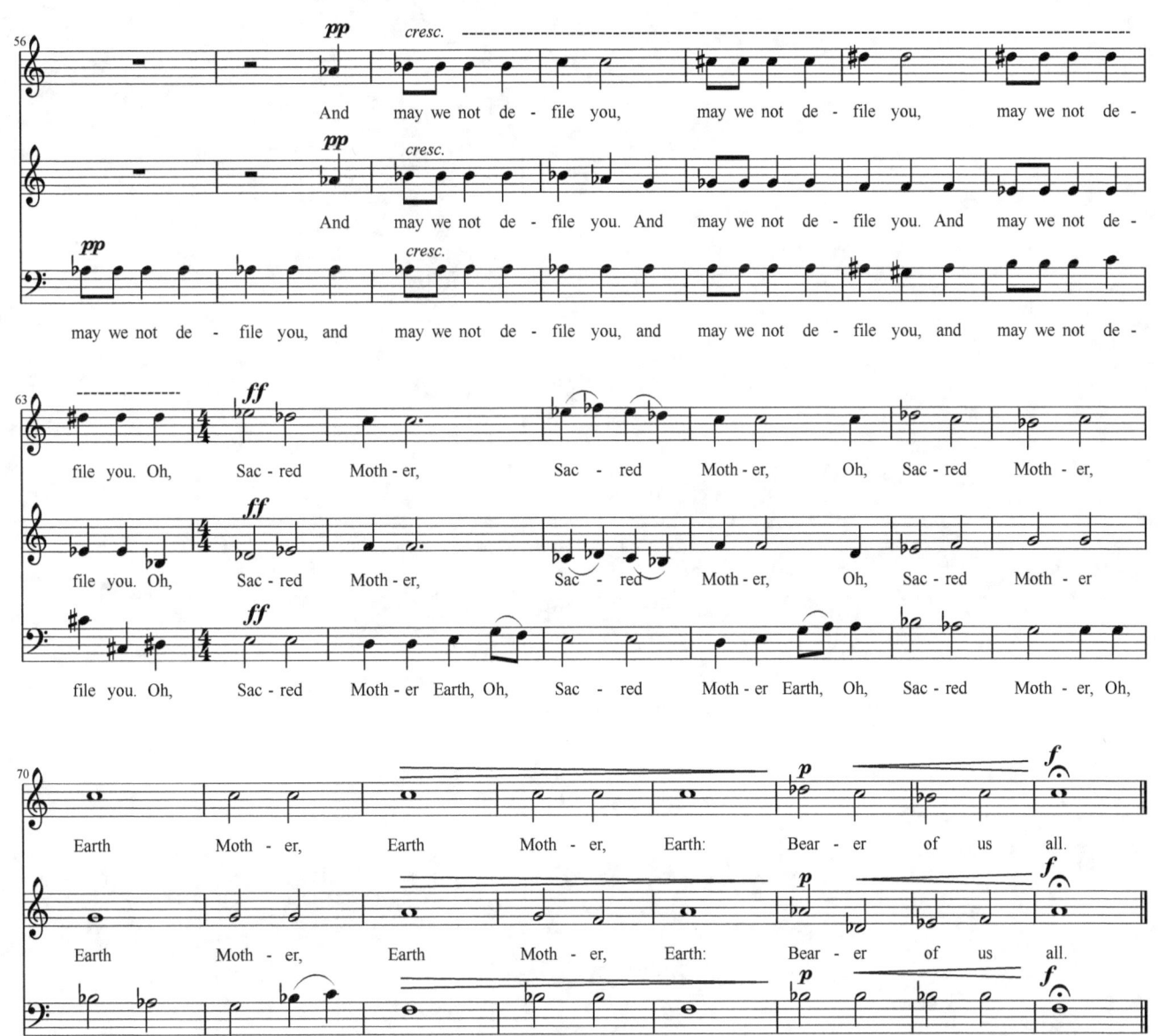

Sacred Dawn

Ken Langer

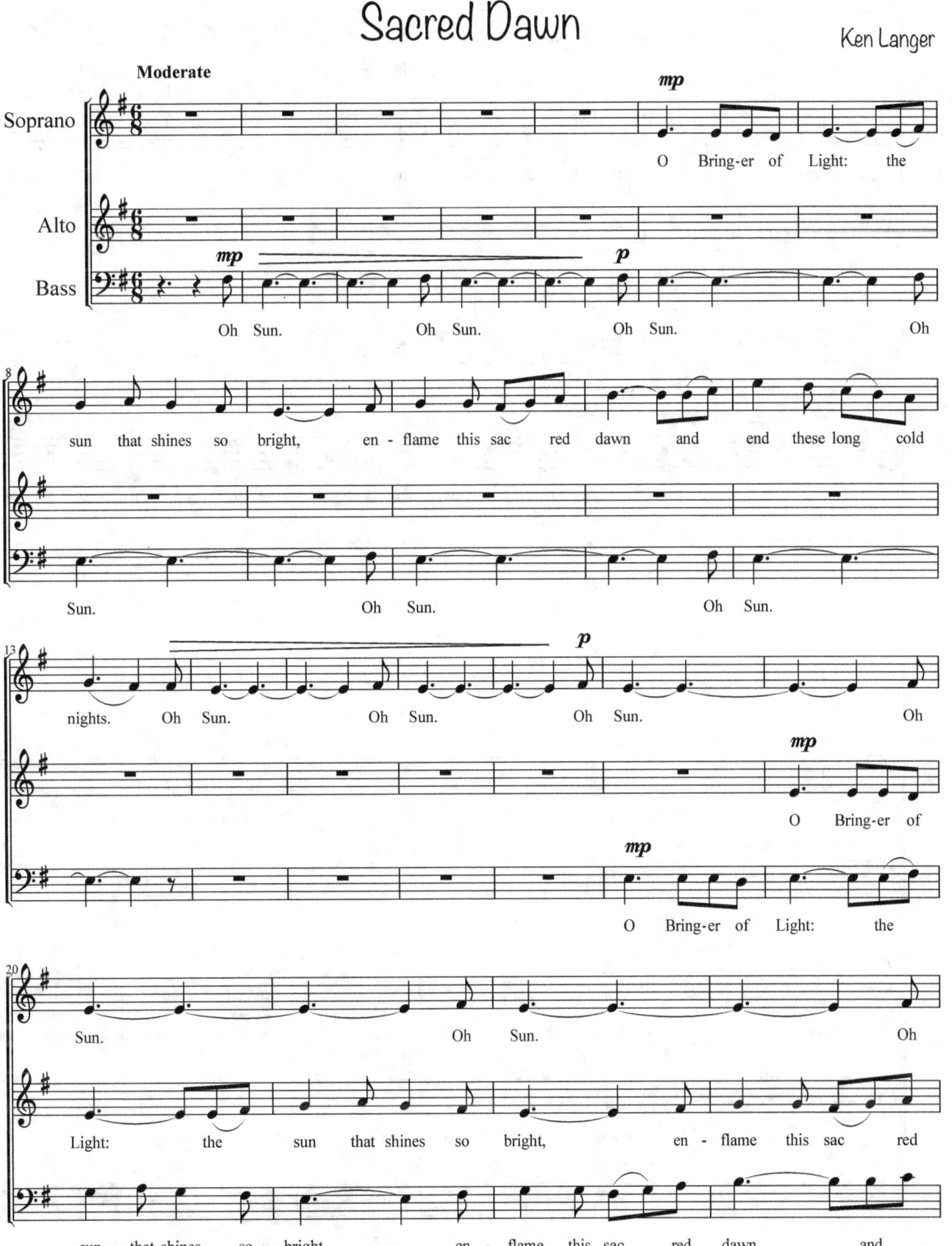

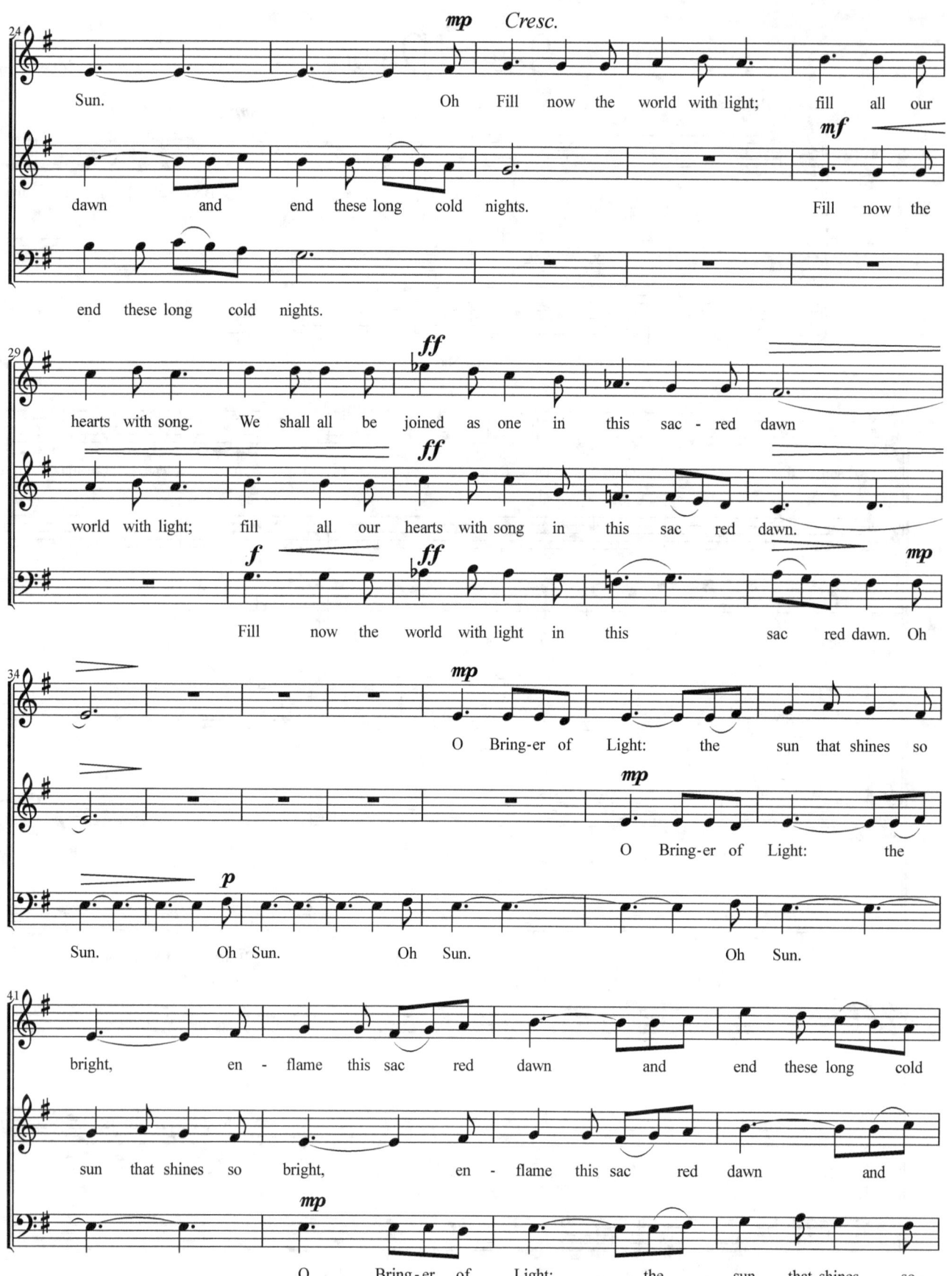

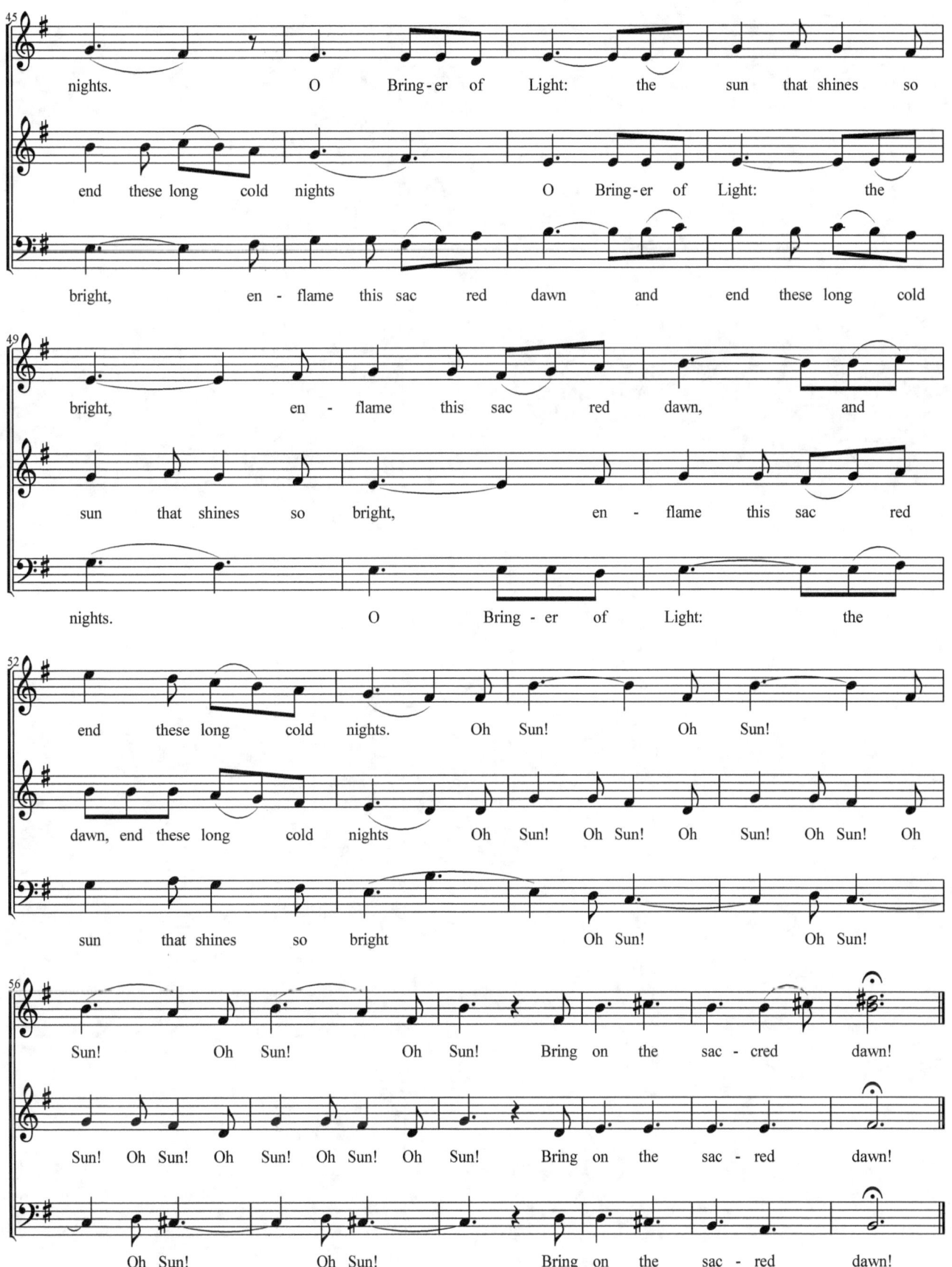

Thirteen Rounds and Canons

Table Of Contents

Notes:
The difference between a round and a canon in this collection is that a round is a single line of music that is meant to be repeated at different times while a canon is written out and has some changes to the polyphonic lines to create a complete piece.

Rounds should be performed by having the next entrance done when the first group reaches the first double bar. For example, if there is a double bar at measure 3, the first group would being and when it reached measure 3 the next group should start at the beginning until all groups (whose number is indicated in the subtitle) have entered.

Around The Circle

(a four part round)

Ken Langer

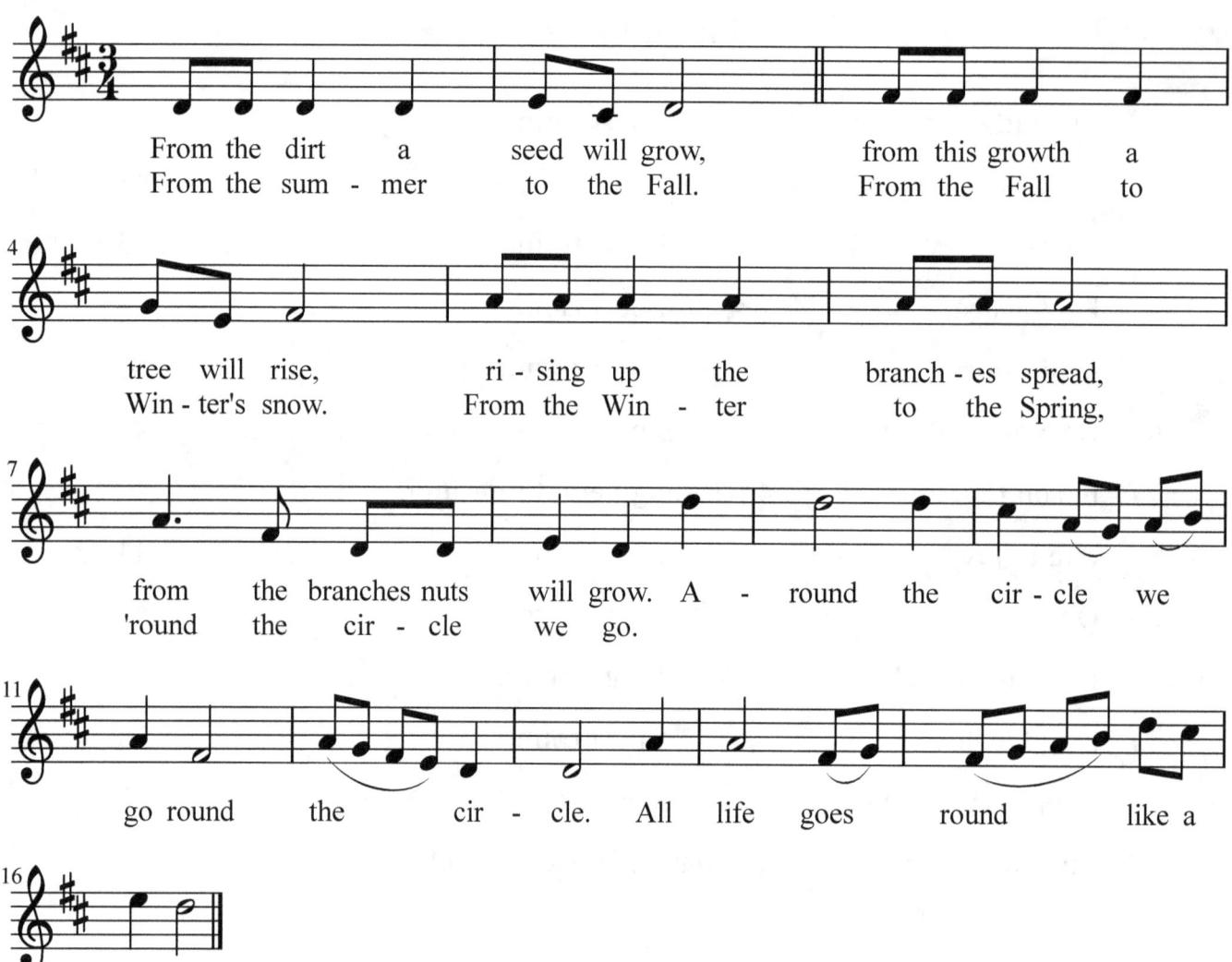

From the dirt   a   seed will grow,   from this growth   a
From the sum - mer   to   the Fall.   From the Fall   to

tree will rise,   ri - sing up   the   branch - es spread,
Win - ter's snow.   From the Win - ter   to   the Spring,

from   the branches nuts   will grow. A -   round   the   cir - cle   we
'round   the   cir - cle   we   go.

go round   the   cir - cle. All   life   goes   round   like a

cir-cle.

A Bright New Day
(a four part double canon)

Ken Langer

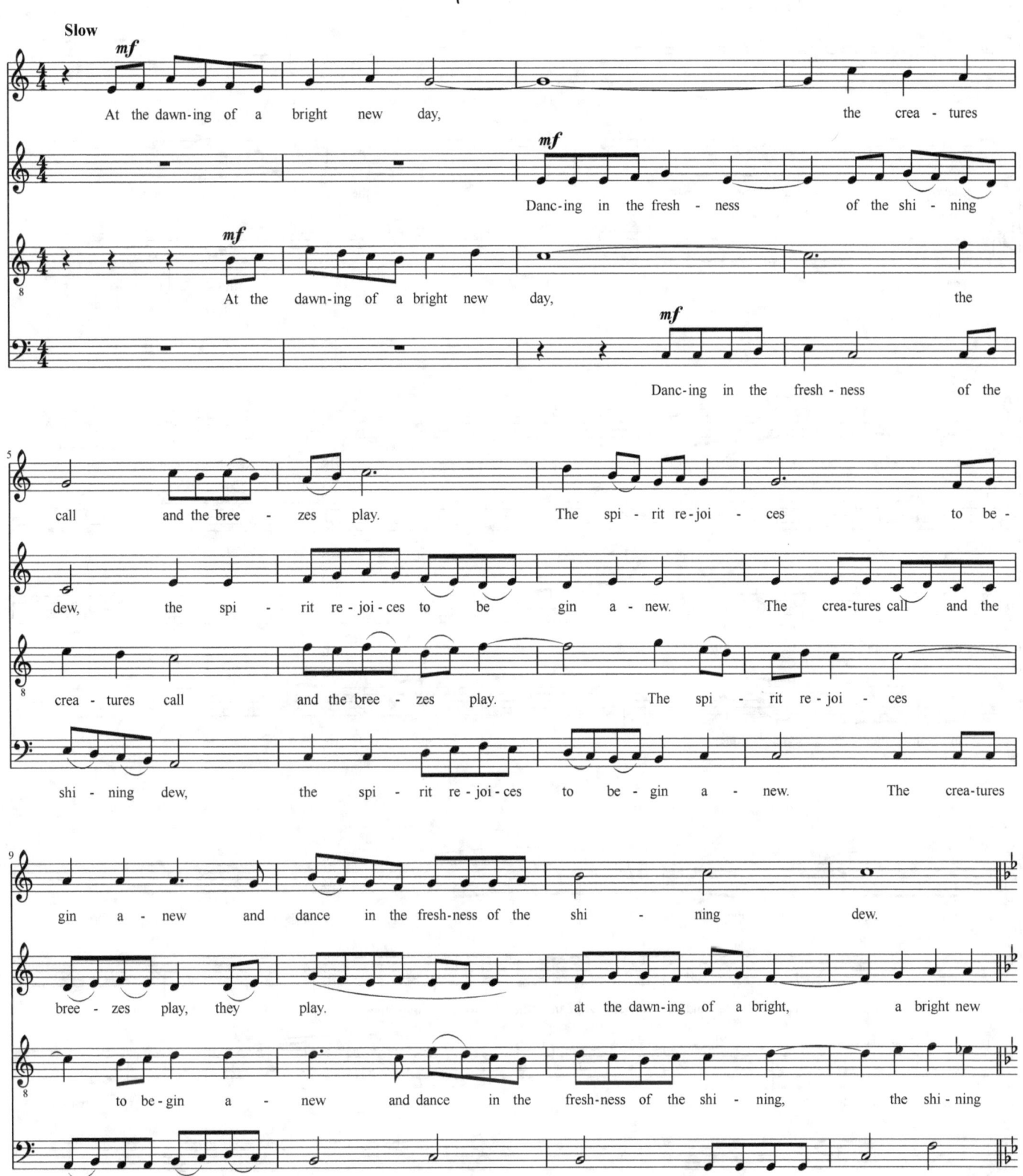

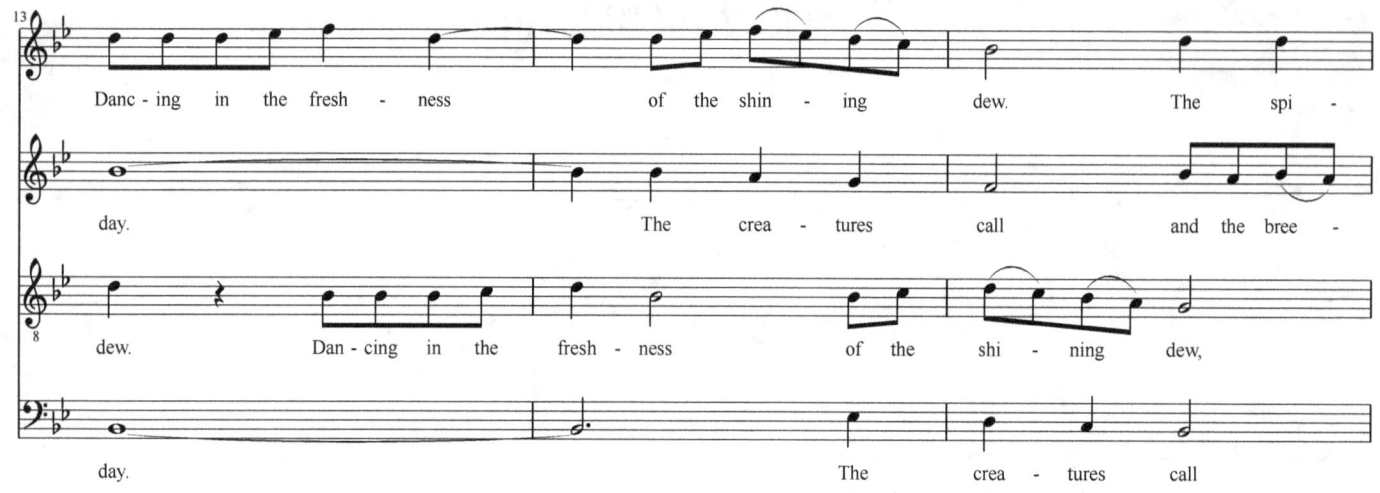

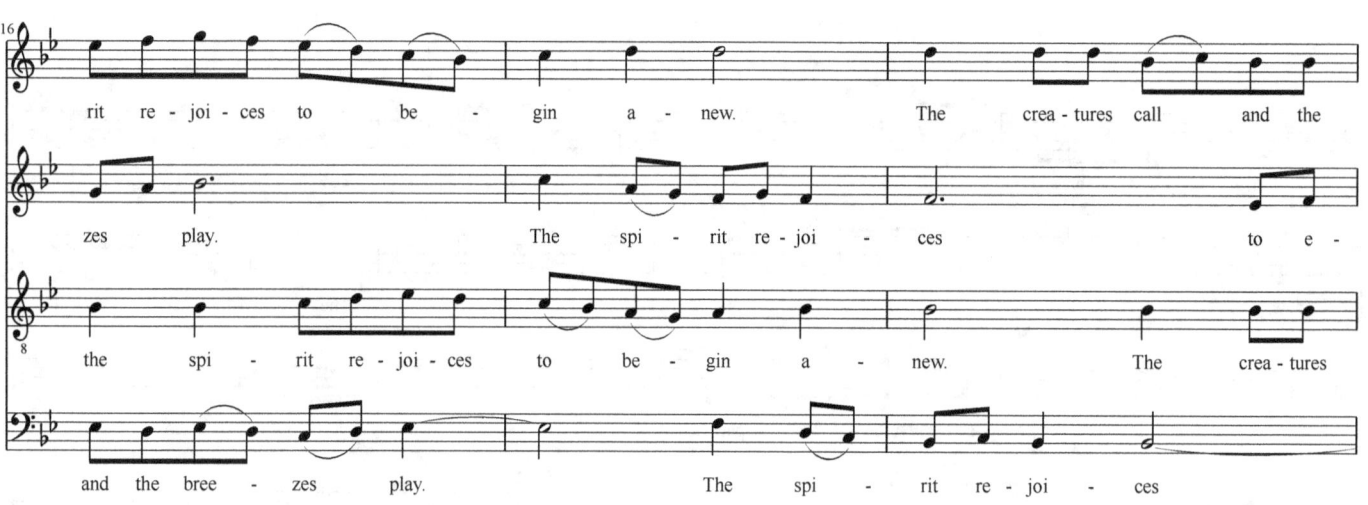

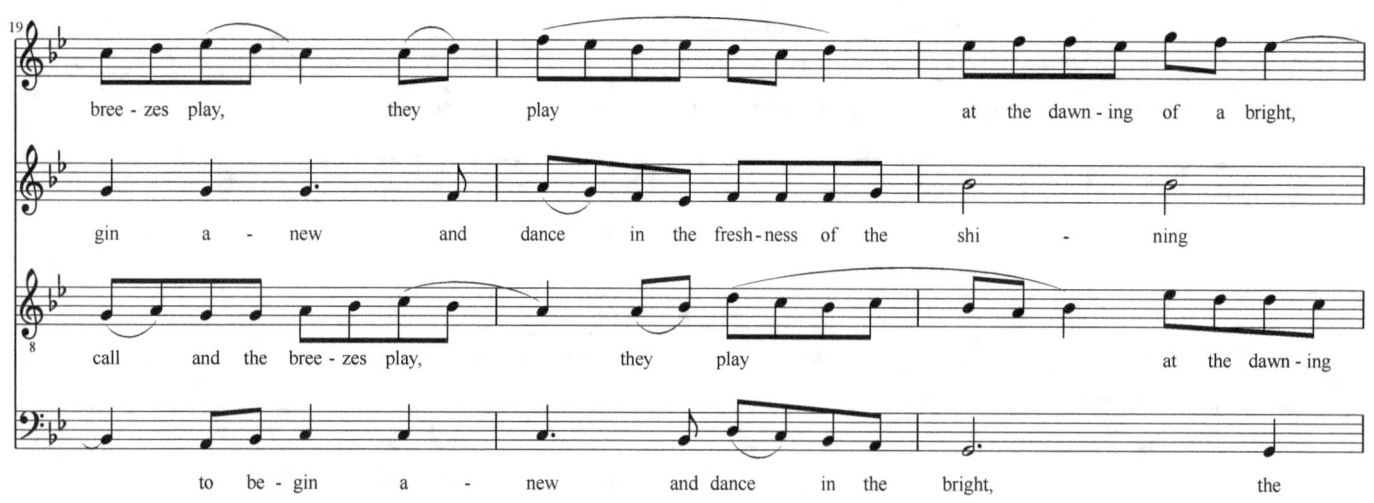

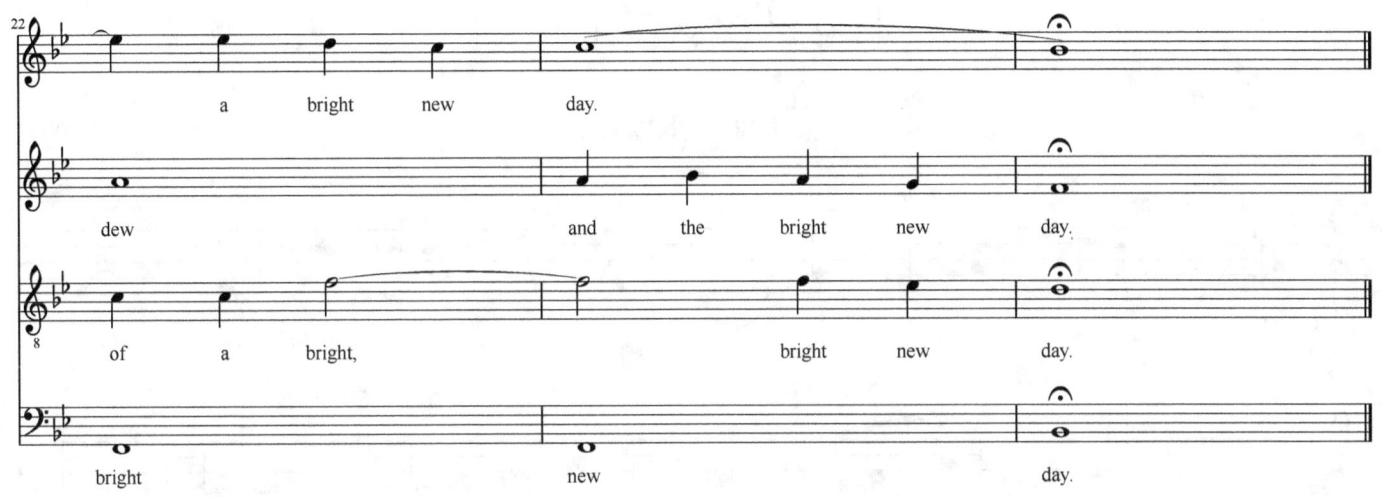

a bright new day.

dew and the bright new day.

of a bright, bright new day.

bright new day.

The Close of Day

(a four part round)

Ken Langer

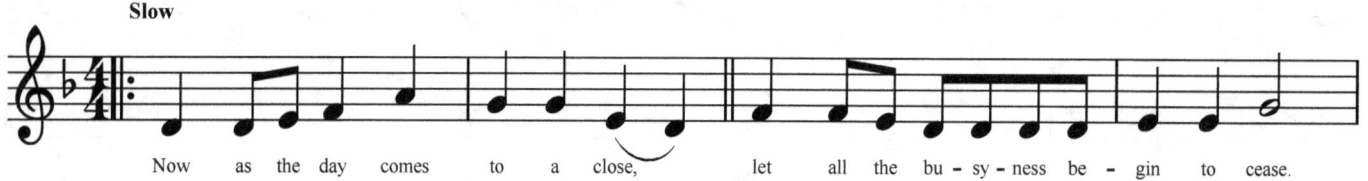

Now   as   the   day   comes   to   a   close,   let   all   the   bu – sy – ness   be – gin   to   cease.

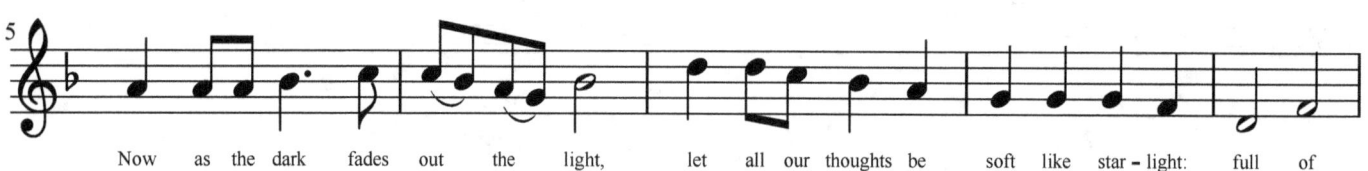

Now   as   the   dark   fades   out   the   light,   let   all   our   thoughts   be   soft   like   star – light: full   of

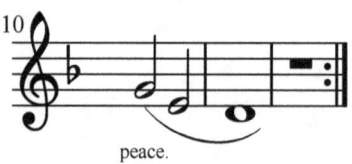

peace.

Find Peace
(a four part canon)

Ken Langer

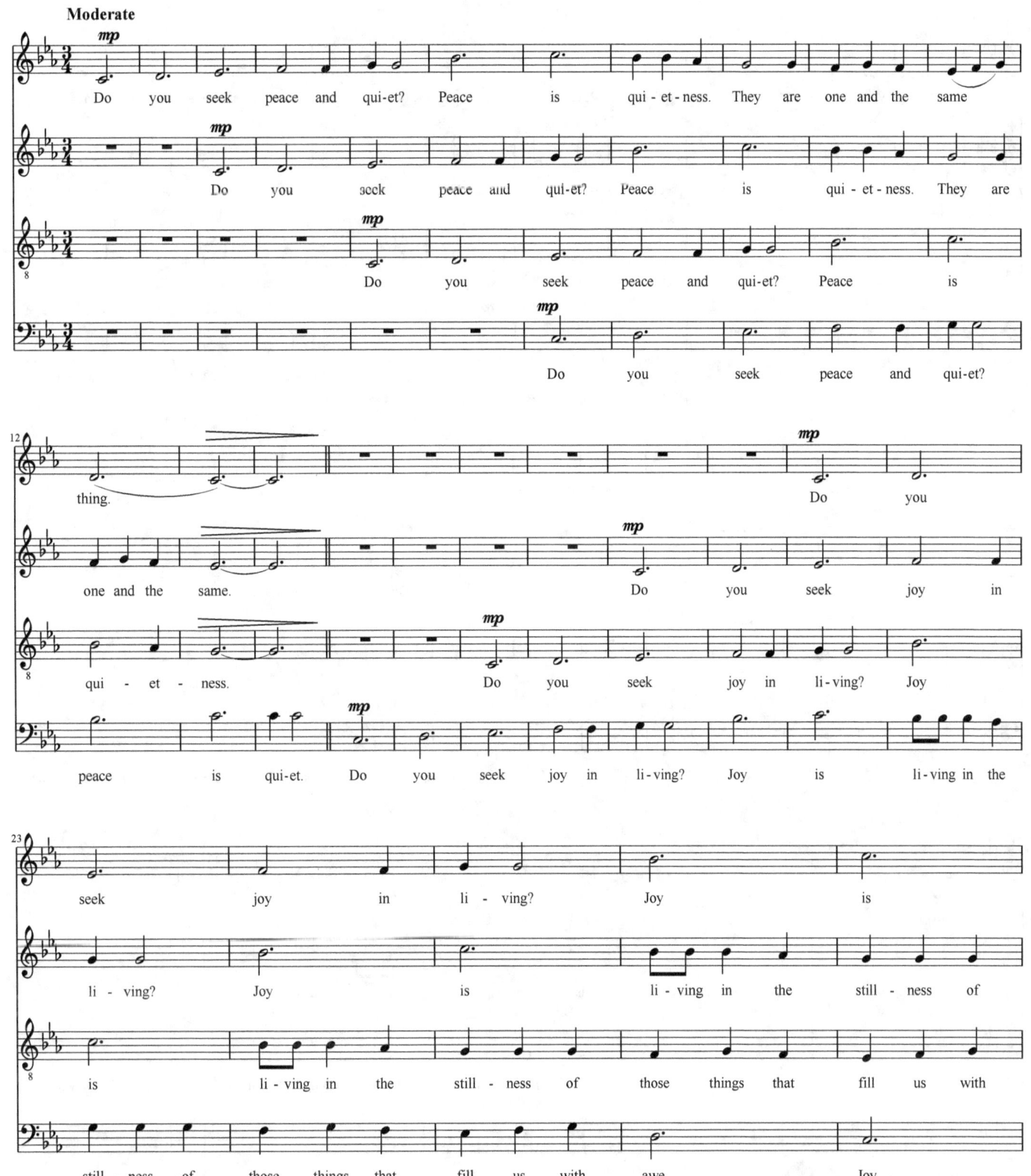

Find Peace
(a four part canon)

Ken Langer

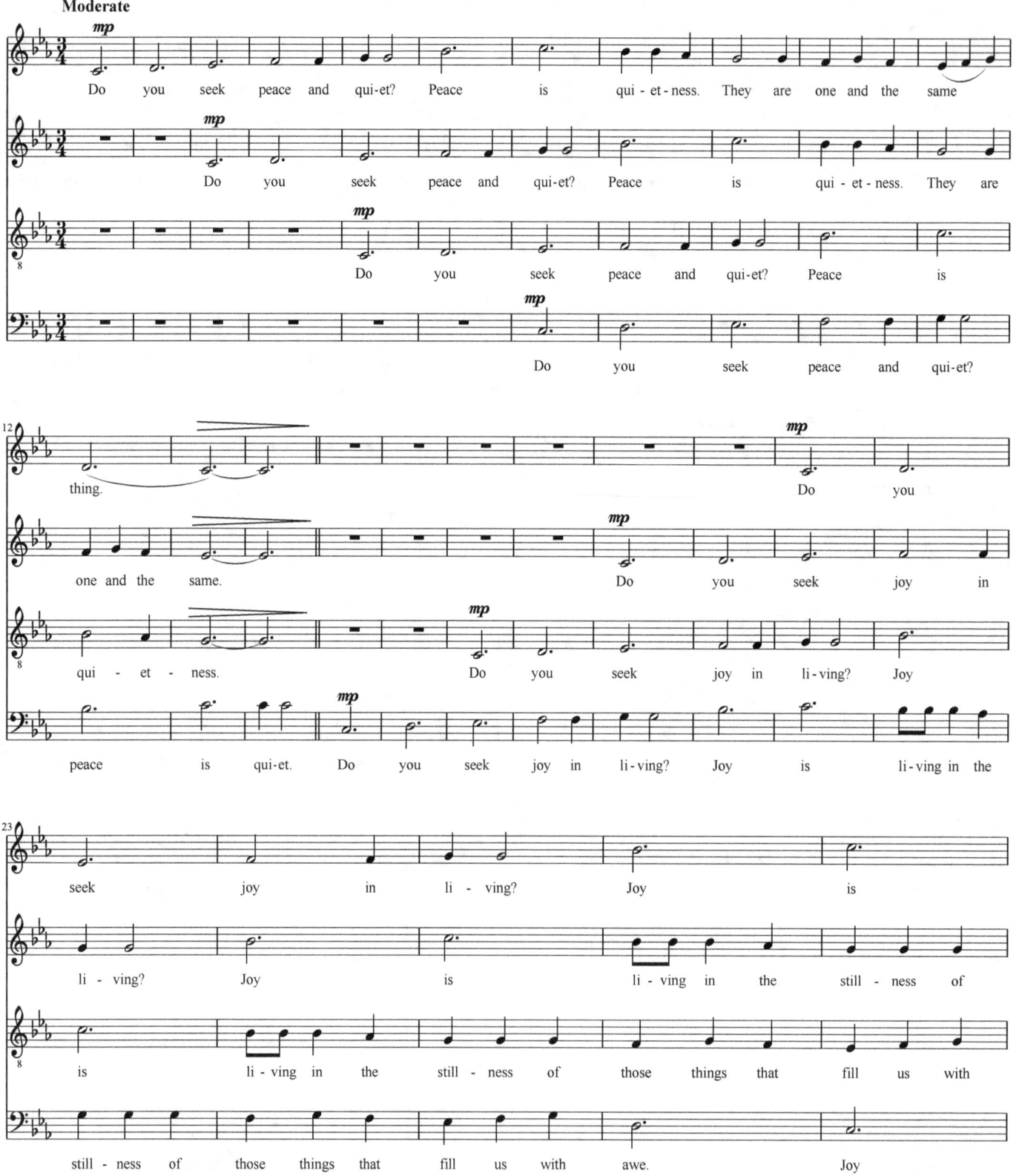

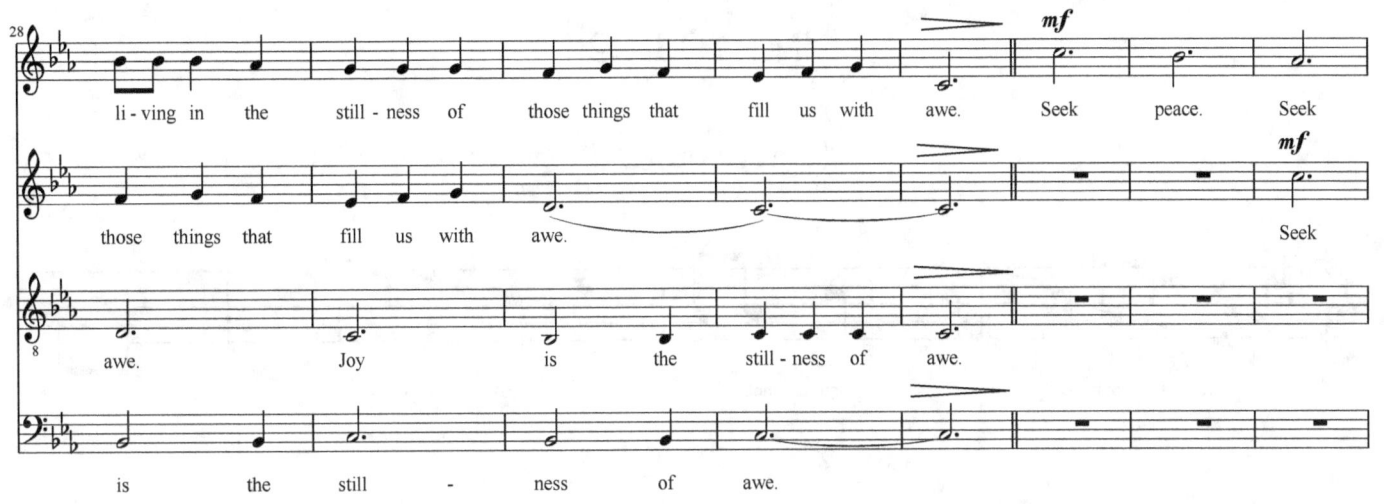

living in the still-ness of those things that fill us with awe. Seek peace. Seek

those things that fill us with awe. Seek

awe. Joy is the still-ness of awe.

is the still-ness of awe.

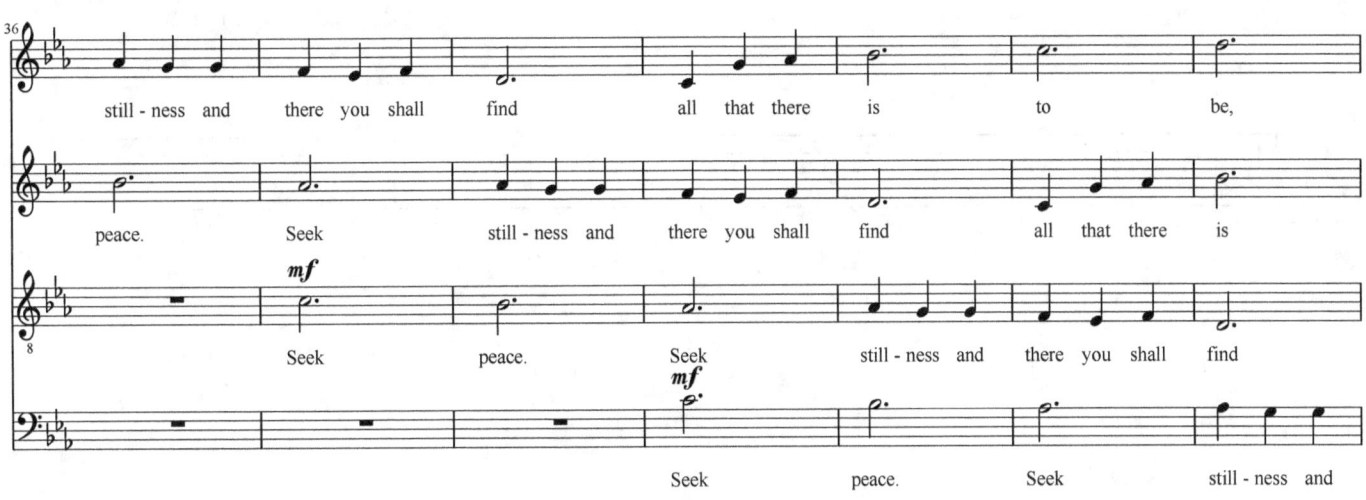

still-ness and there you shall find all that there is to be,

peace. Seek still-ness and there you shall find all that there is

Seek peace. Seek still-ness and there you shall find

Seek peace. Seek still-ness and

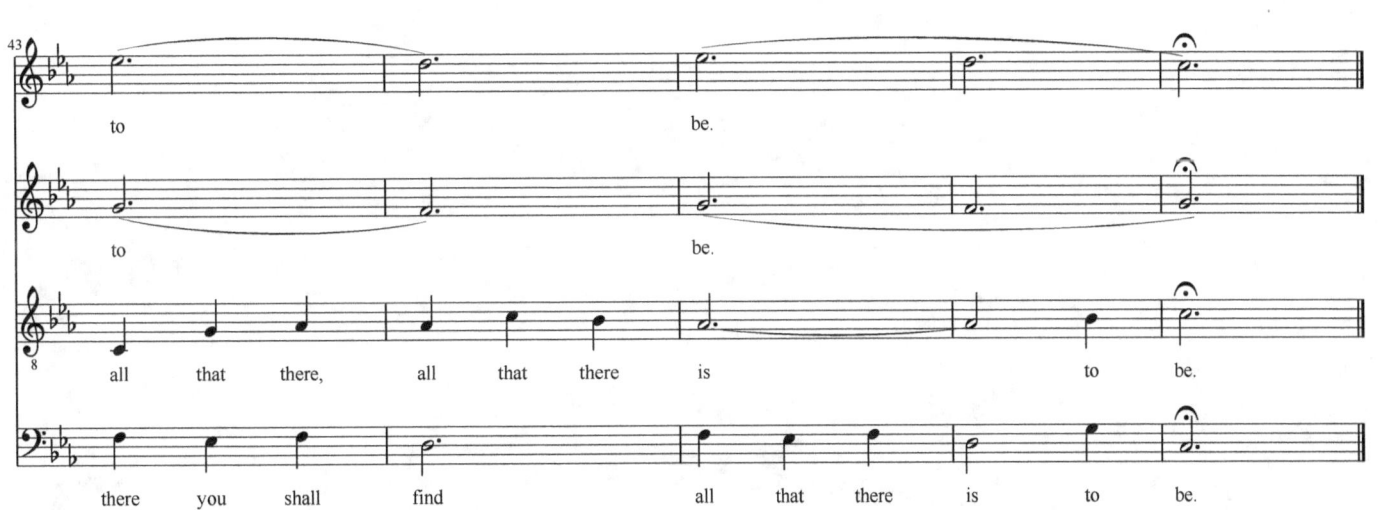

to be.

to be.

all that there, all that there is to be.

there you shall find all that there is to be.

Find Yourself

(a three part round)

Ken Langer

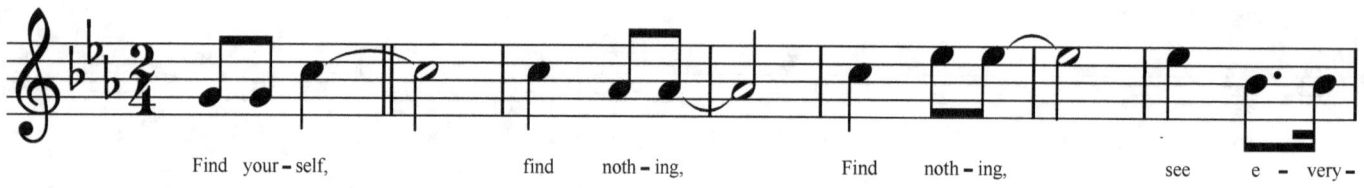

Find your-self, find noth-ing, Find noth-ing, see e-very-

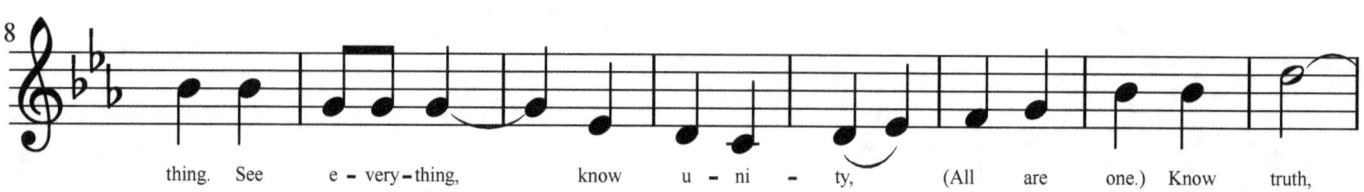

thing. See e-very-thing, know u-ni-ty, (All are one.) Know truth,

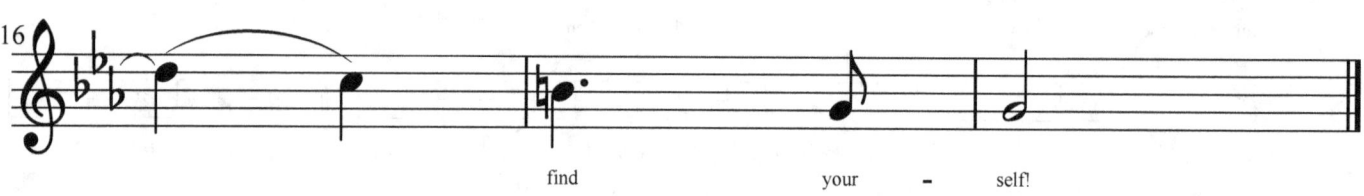

find your-self!

Go Now In Peace

Ken Langer

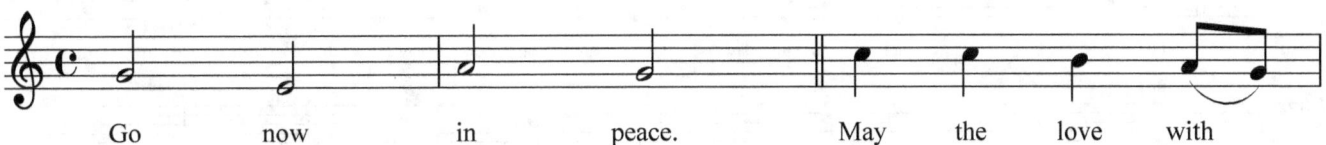

Go   now   in   peace.   May   the   love   with

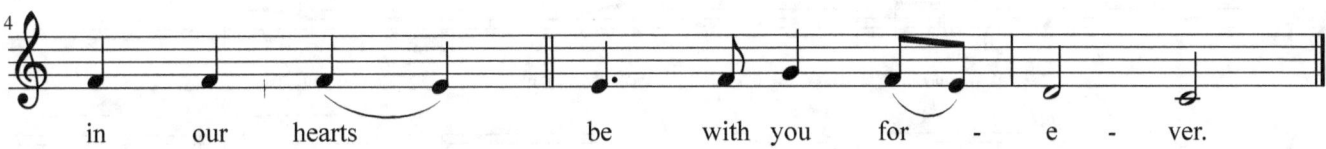

in   our   hearts   be   with   you   for -   e -   ver.

If You Can Live
(a four part augmentation canon)

Ken Langer

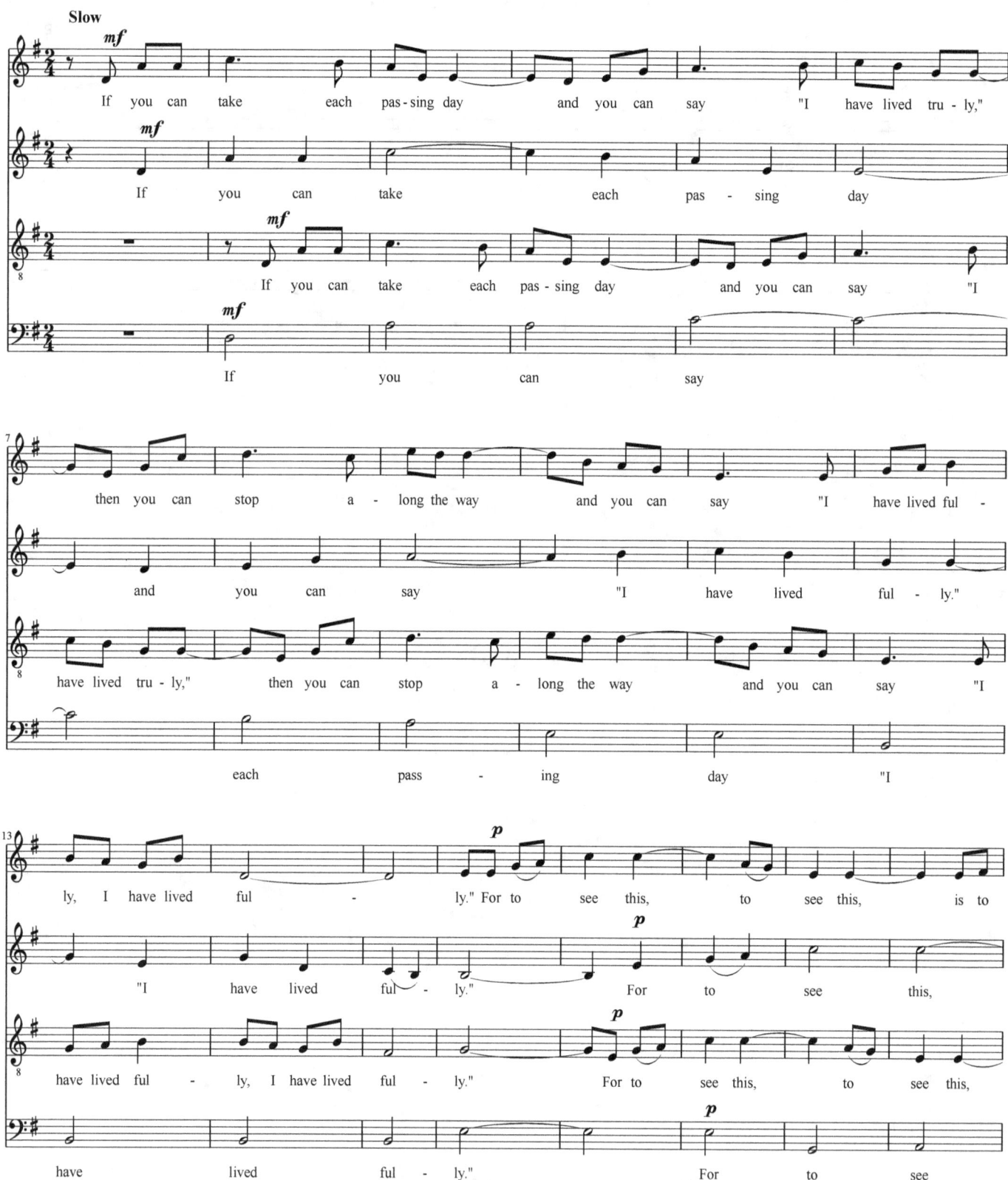

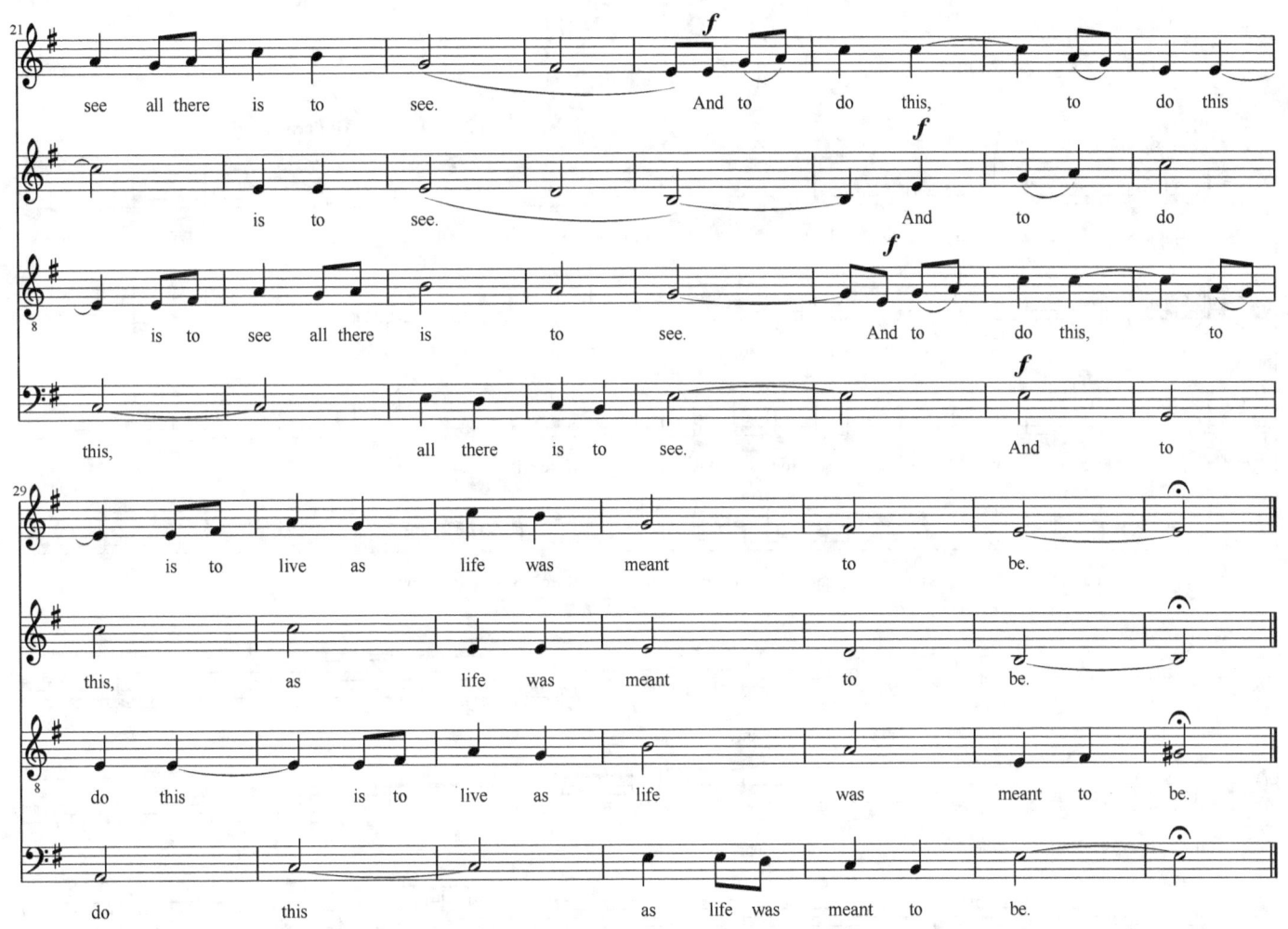

see all there is to see. And to do this, to do this

is to see. And to do

is to see all there is to see. And to do this, to

this, all there is to see. And to

is to live as life was meant to be.

this, as life was meant to be.

do this is to live as life was meant to be.

do this as life was meant to be.

Life Is Joy
(a four part canon)

Ken Langer

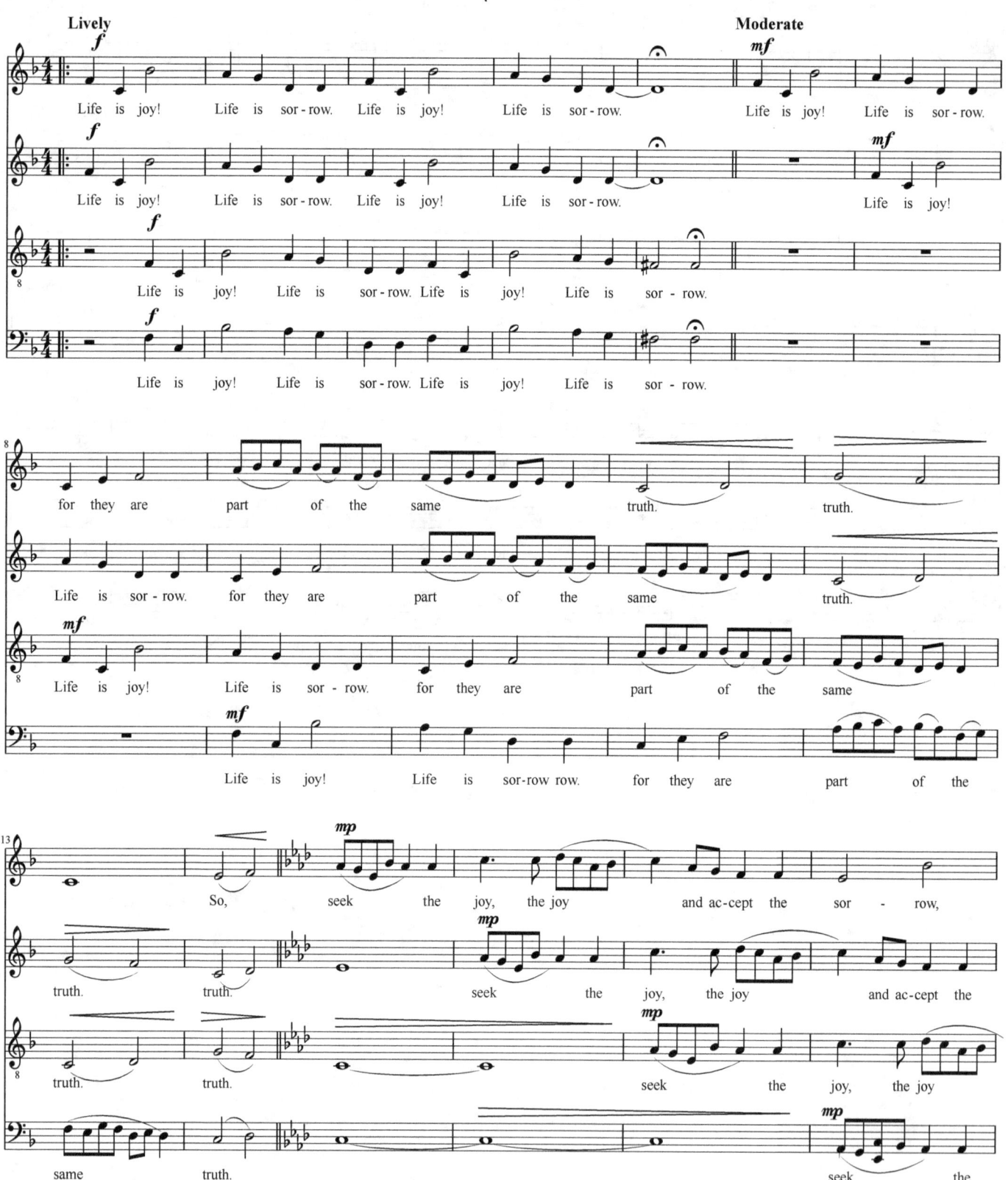

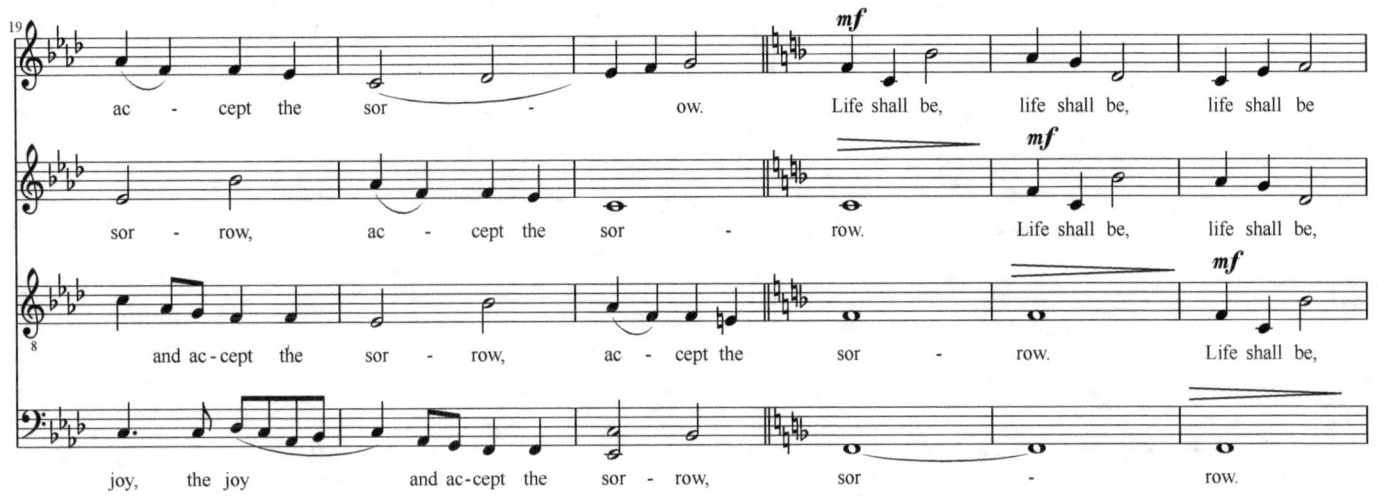

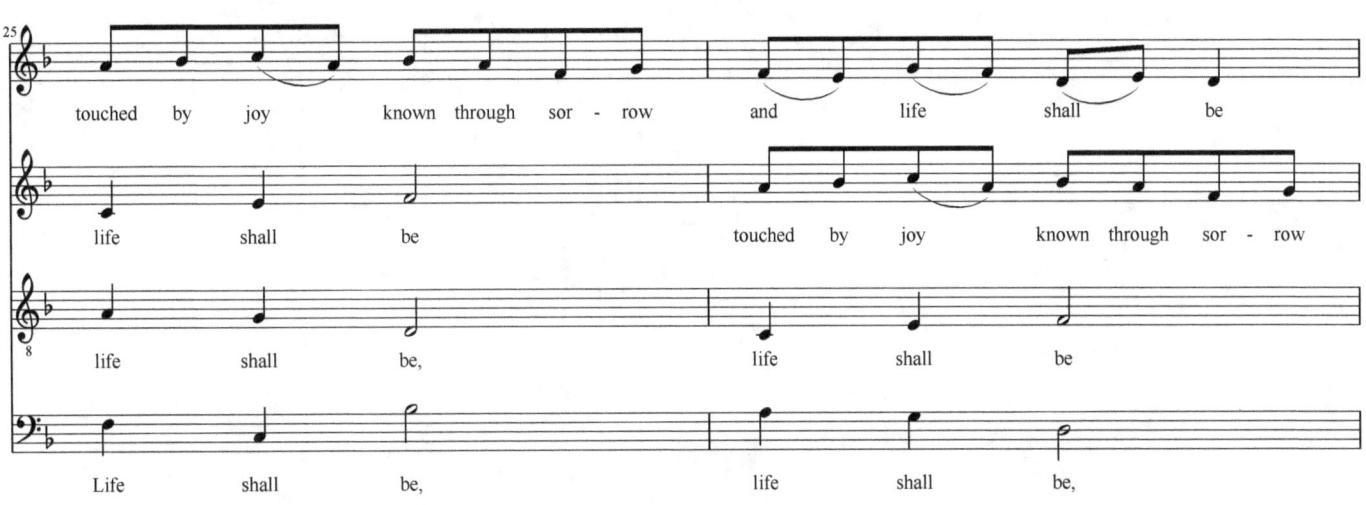

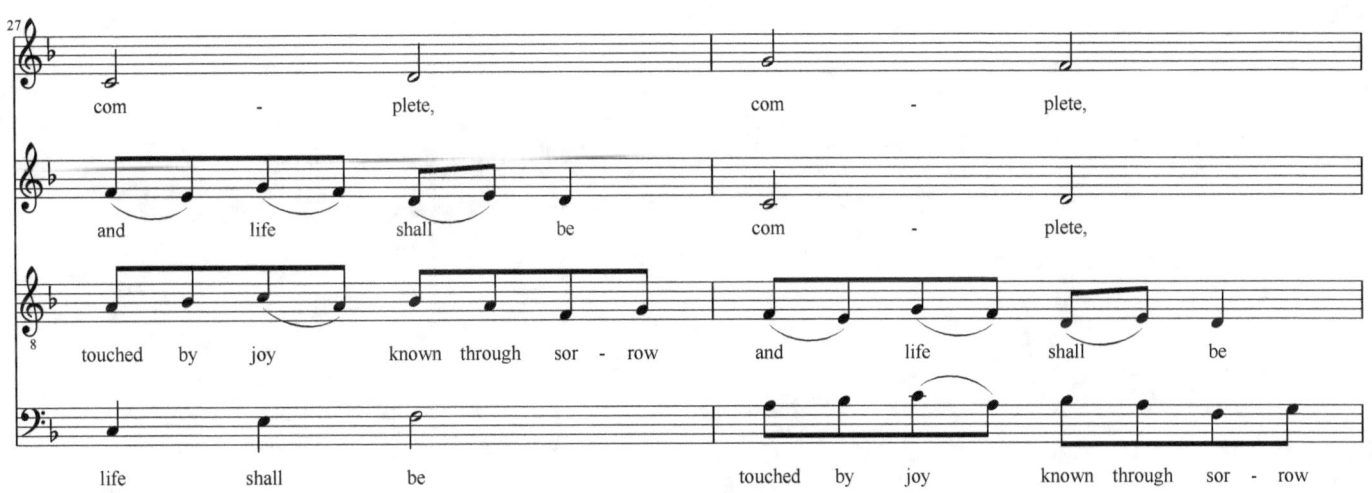

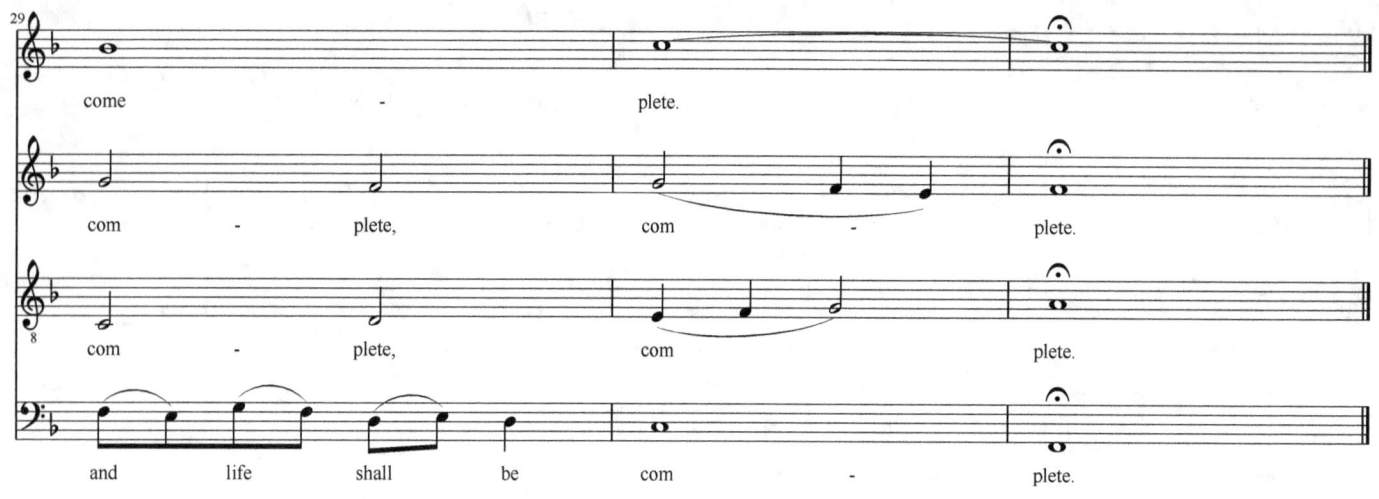

come - plete.

com - plete, com - plete.

com - plete, com - plete.

and life shall be com - plete.

Our Conductor
(a four part catch)

Ken Langer

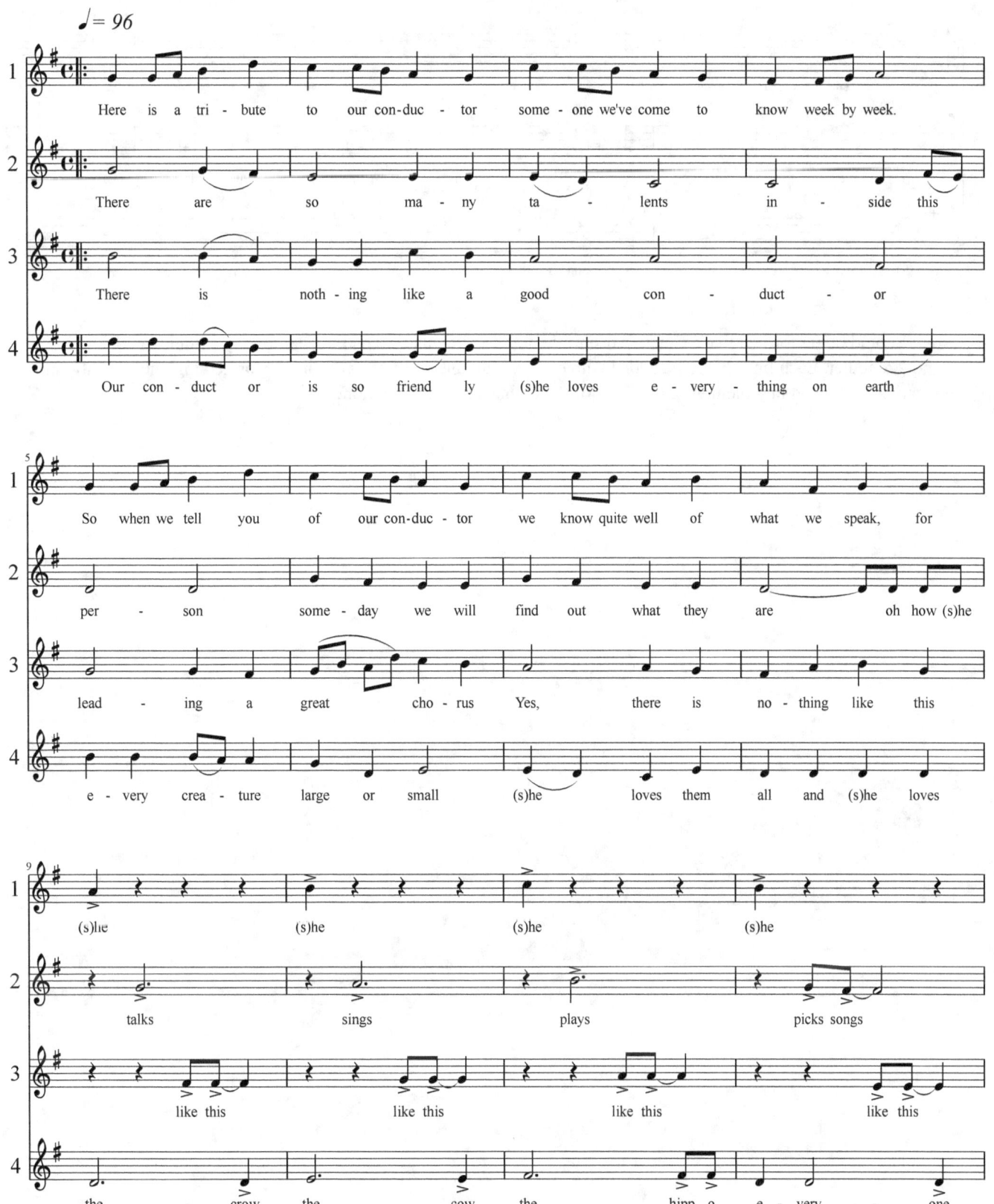

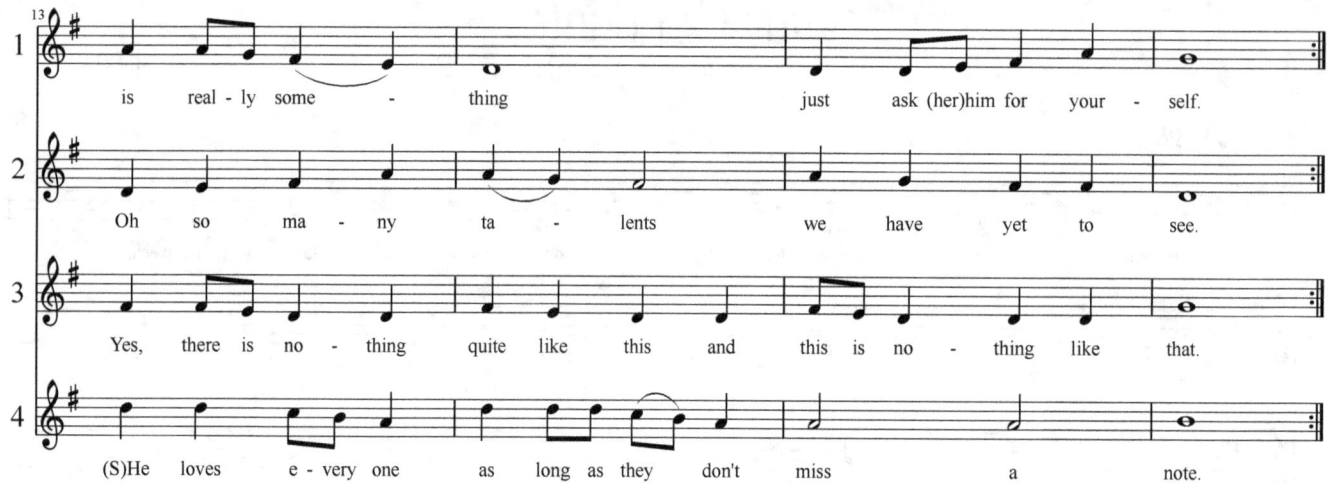

Note: Should be performed like a Catch. All start the top line in unison. Then, repeat to the beginning and sing lines 1 and 2 together. Each line should be added with each repeat until all four parts are performed together. Additional fun can be had by adding pictures and sounds of the animals that are mentioned.

The Rhythms of Life
(a written-out three part round)

Ken Langer

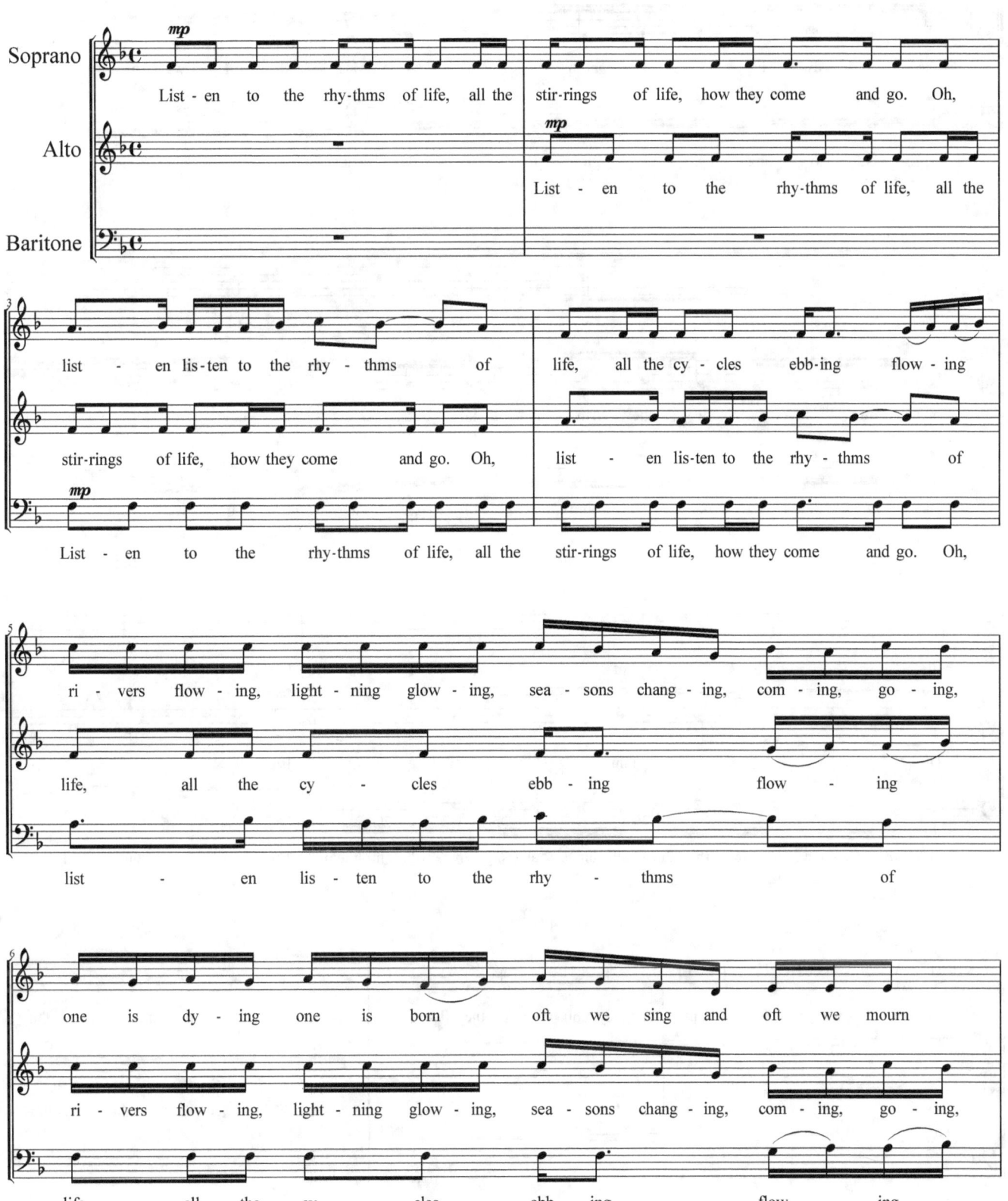

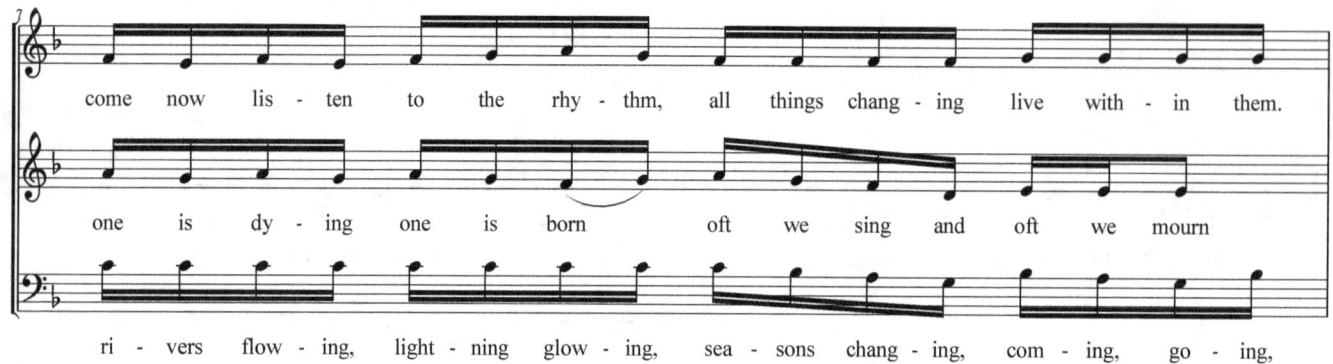

come now lis - ten to the rhy - thm, all things chang-ing live with - in them.

one is dy - ing one is born oft we sing and oft we mourn

ri - vers flow-ing, light-ning glow-ing, sea - sons chang-ing, com-ing, go-ing,

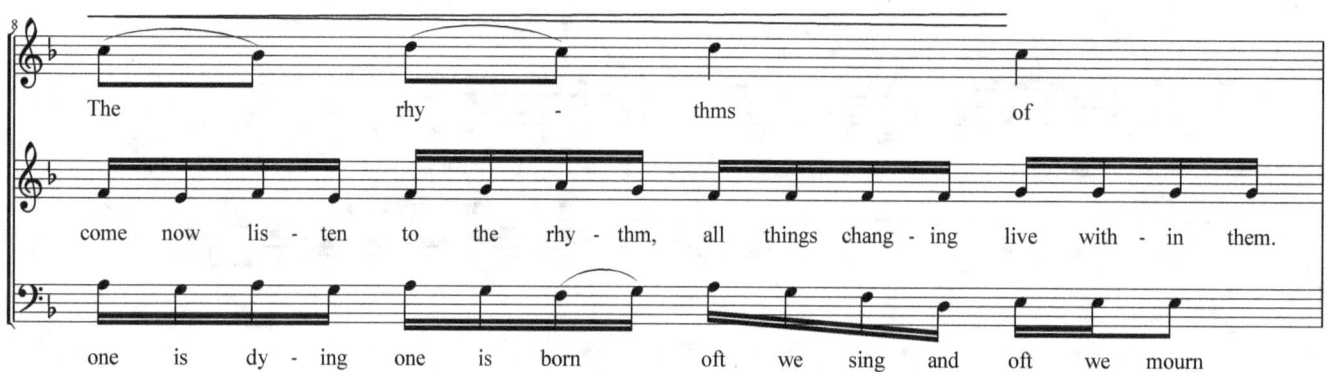

The rhy - thms of

come now lis - ten to the rhy - thm, all things chang-ing live with - in them.

one is dy - ing one is born oft we sing and oft we mourn

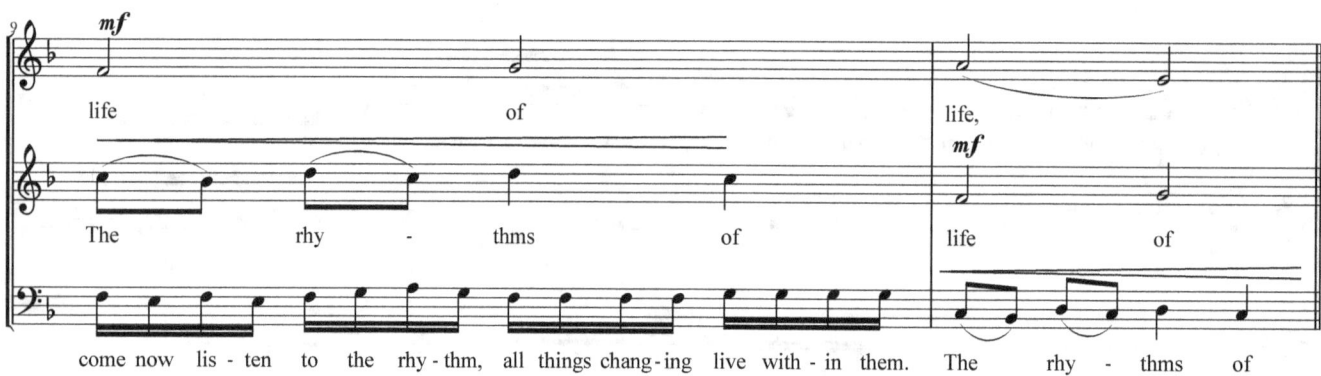

mf

life of life,

mf

The rhy - thms of life of

come now lis - ten to the rhy-thm, all things chang-ing live with-in them. The rhy - thms of

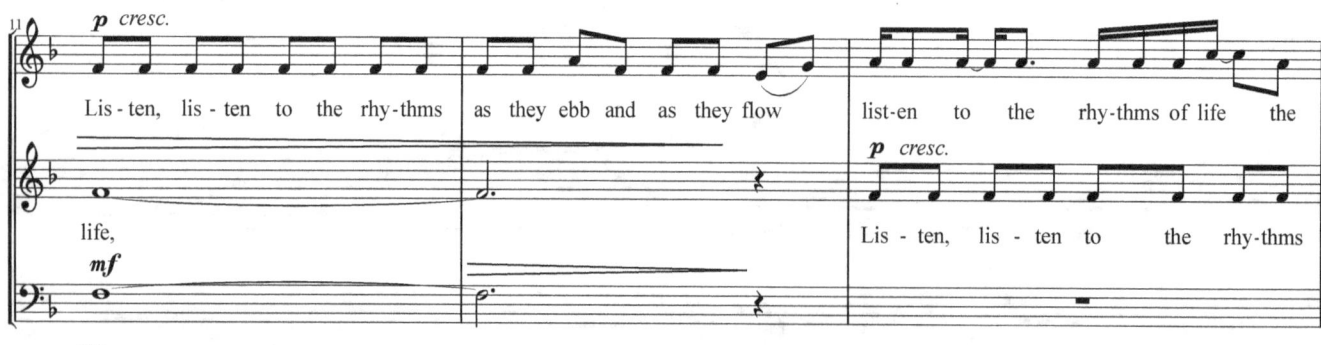

p cresc.

Lis - ten, lis - ten to the rhy-thms as they ebb and as they flow list-en to the rhy-thms of life the

p cresc.

life, Lis - ten, lis - ten to the rhy-thms

mf

life,

life,

50

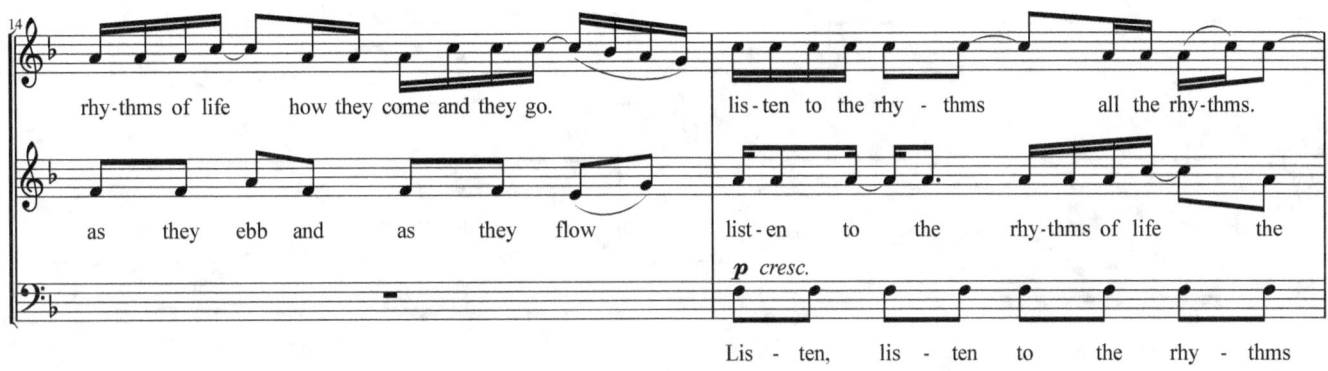

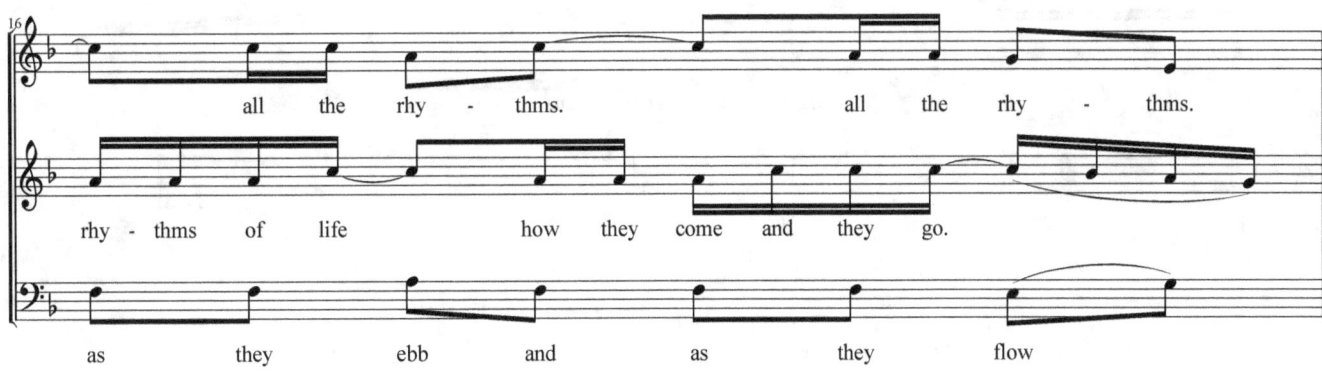

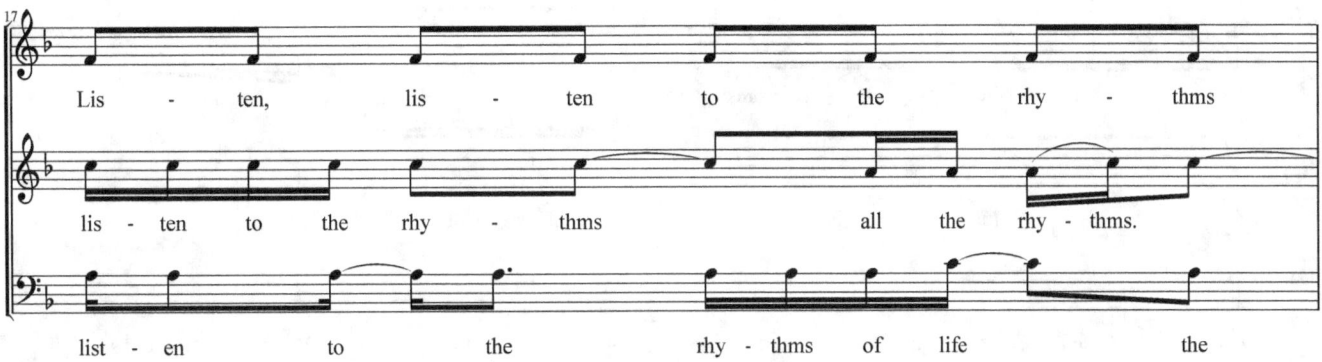

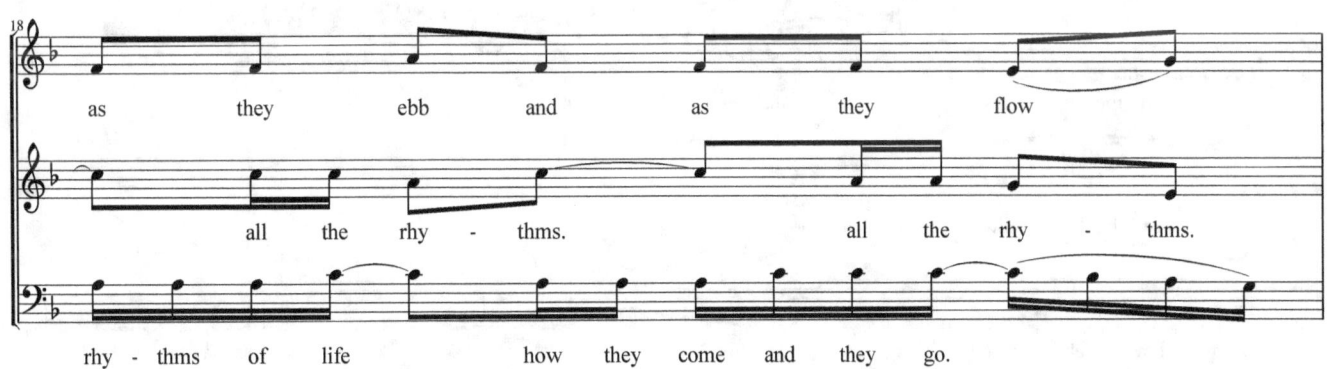

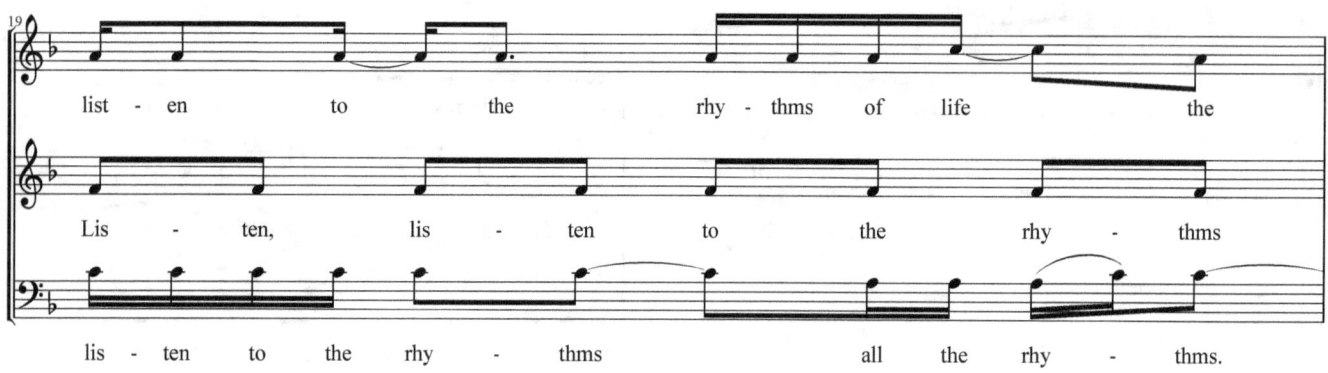

19

Soprano: list - en to the rhy - thms of life the

Alto: Lis - ten, lis - ten to the rhy - thms

Bass: lis - ten to the rhy - thms all the rhy - thms.

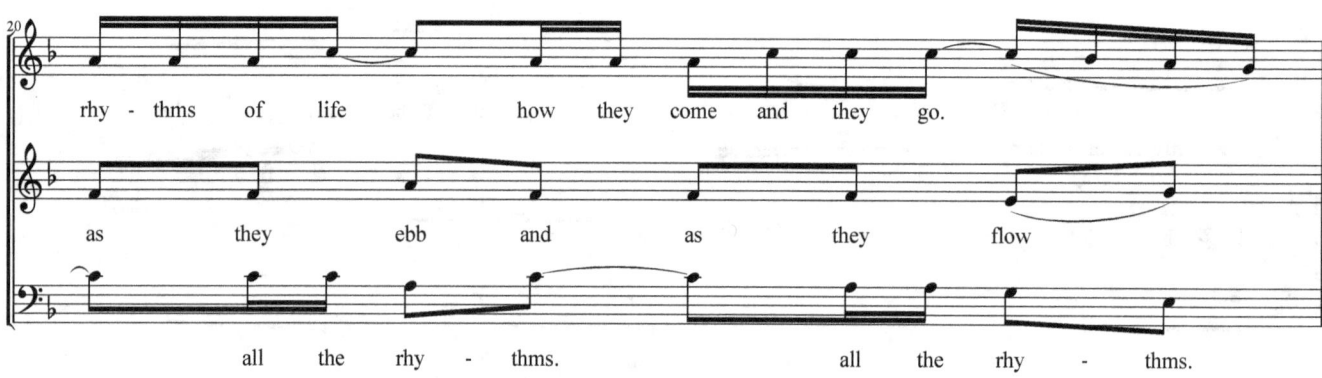

20

Soprano: rhy - thms of life how they come and they go.

Alto: as they ebb and as they flow

Bass: all the rhy - thms. all the rhy - thms.

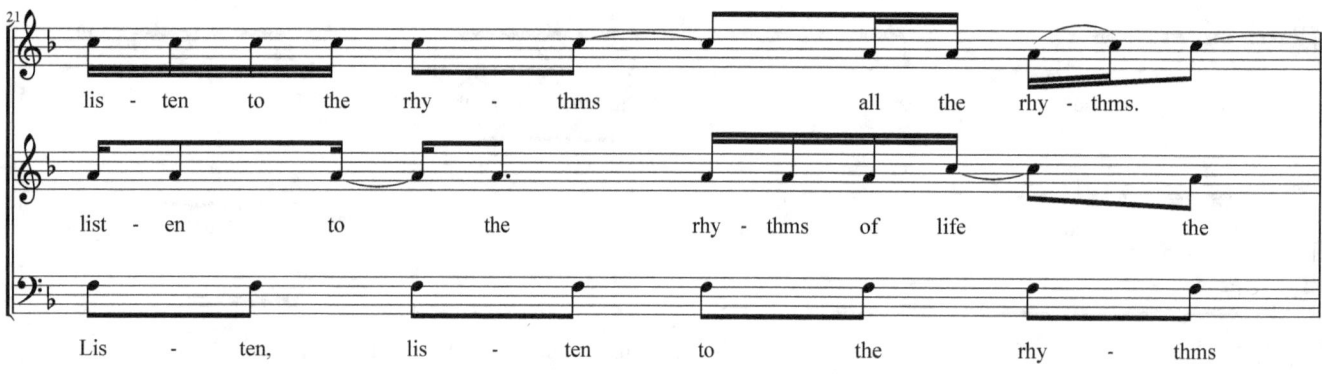

21

Soprano: lis - ten to the rhy - thms all the rhy - thms.

Alto: list - en to the rhy - thms of life the

Bass: Lis - ten, lis - ten to the rhy - thms

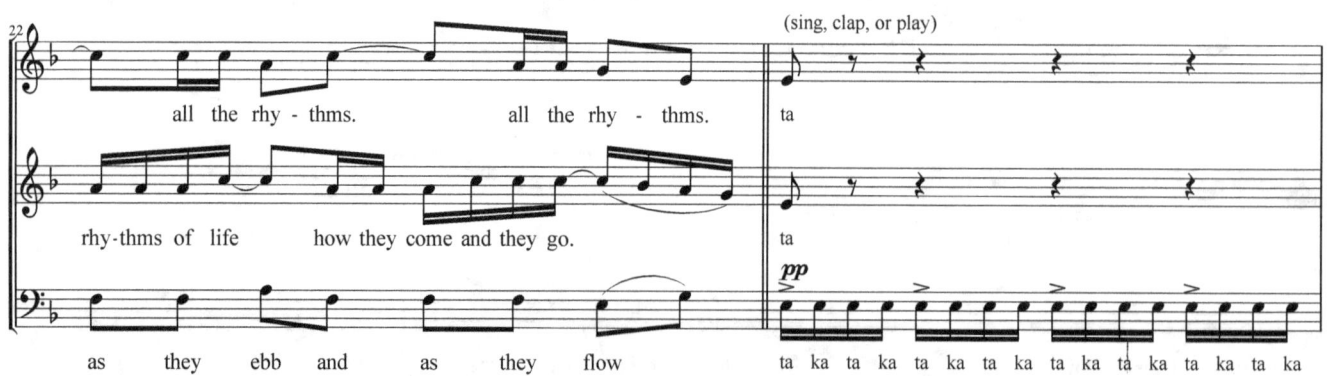

22

(sing, clap, or play)

Soprano: all the rhy - thms. all the rhy - thms. ta

Alto: rhy-thms of life how they come and they go. ta

Bass: as they ebb and as they flow *pp* ta ka ta ka ta ka ta ka ta ka ta ka ta ka ta ka

52

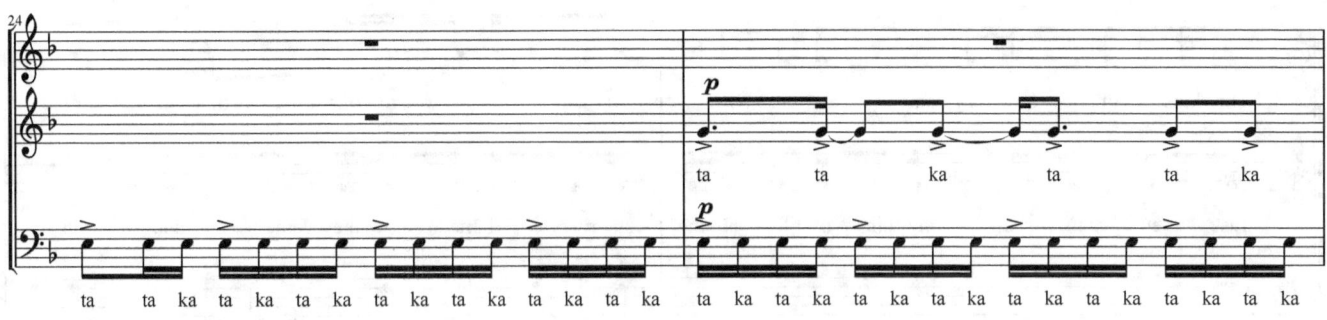

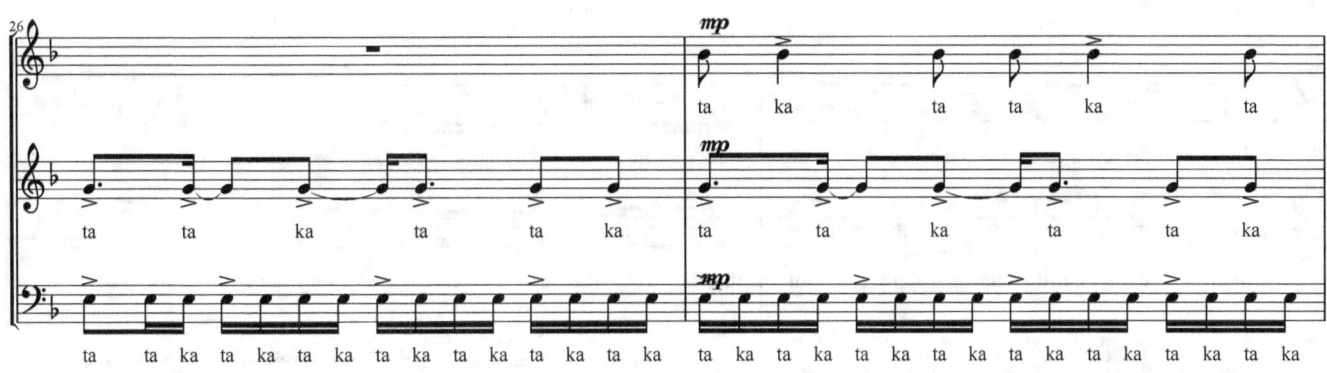

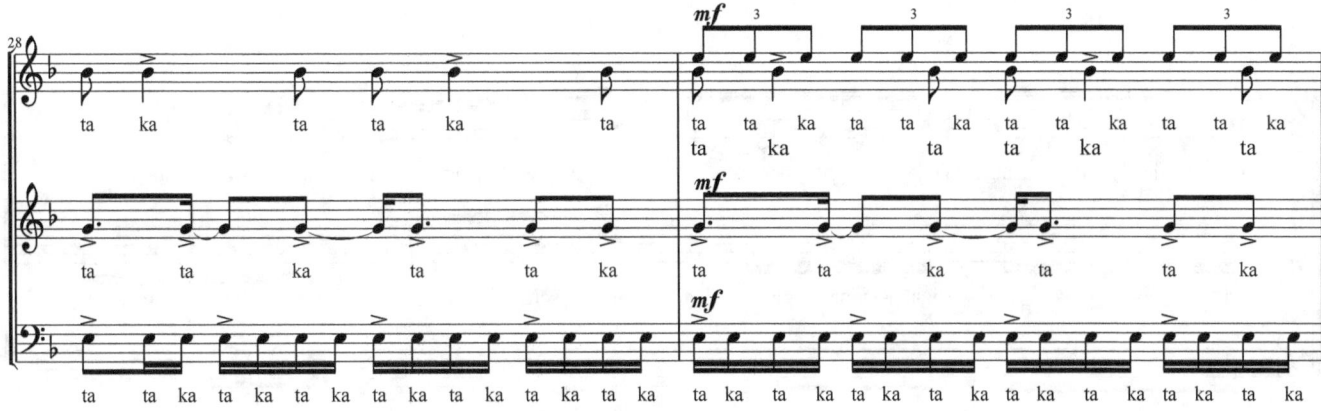

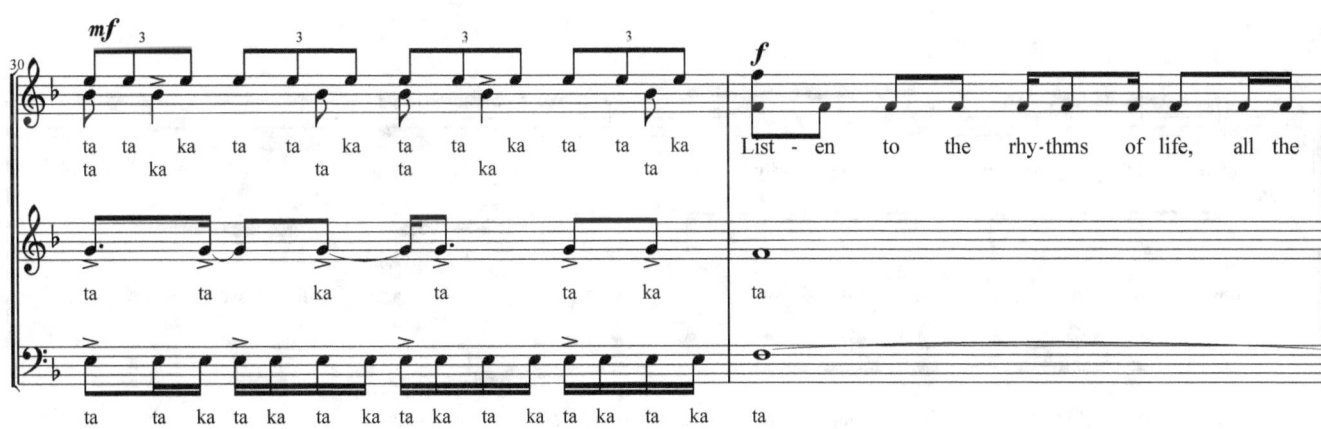

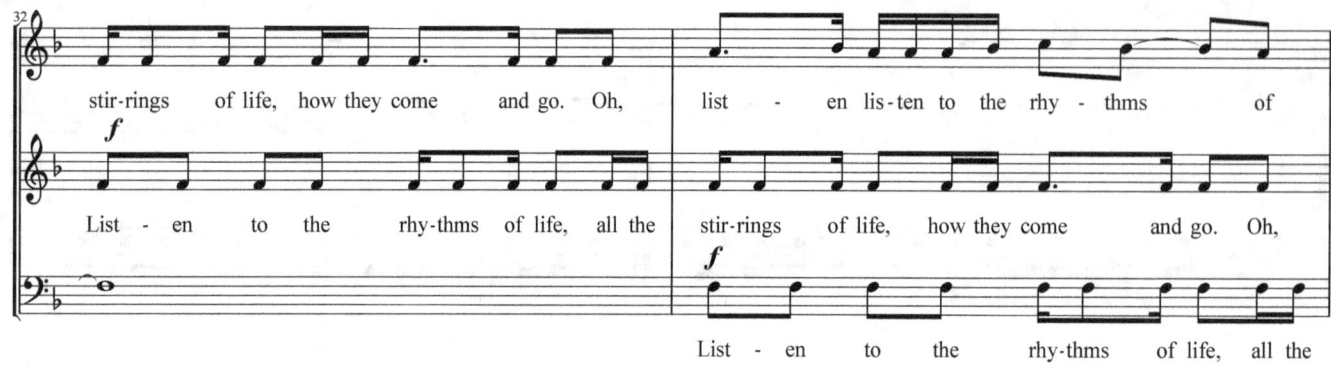

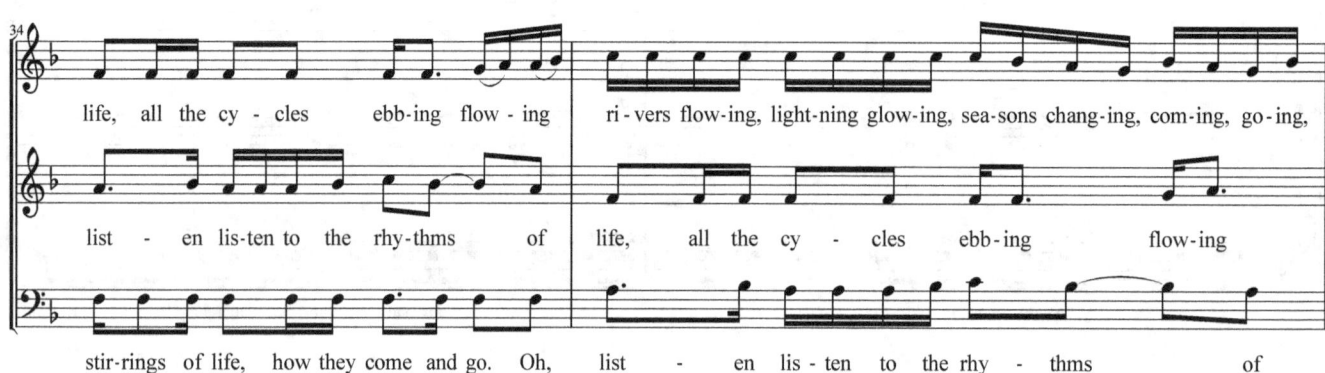

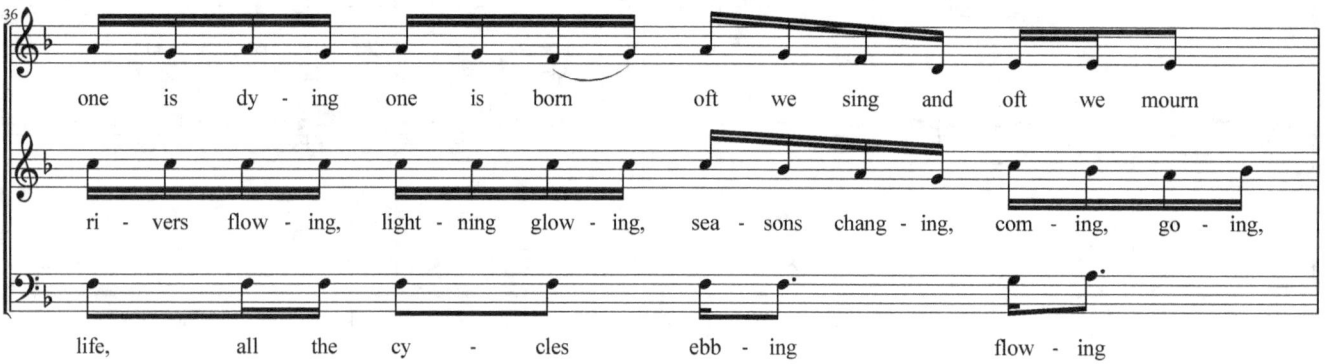

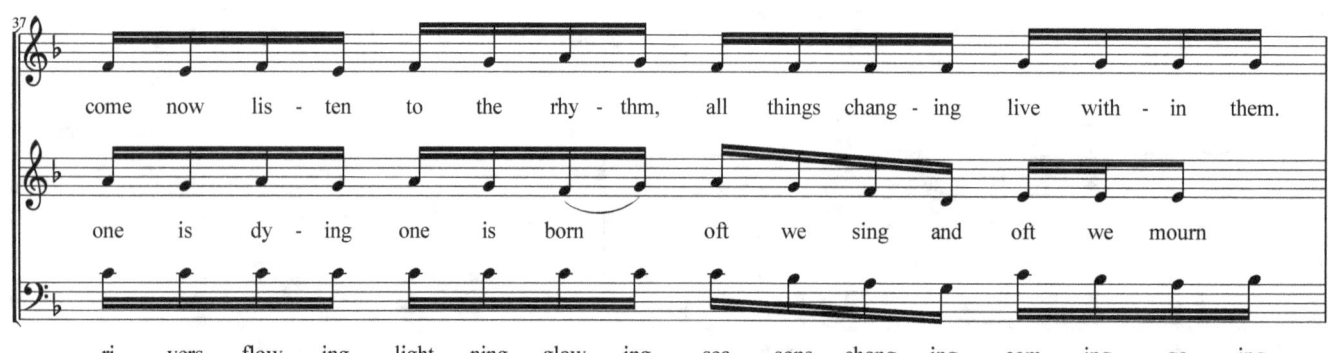

54

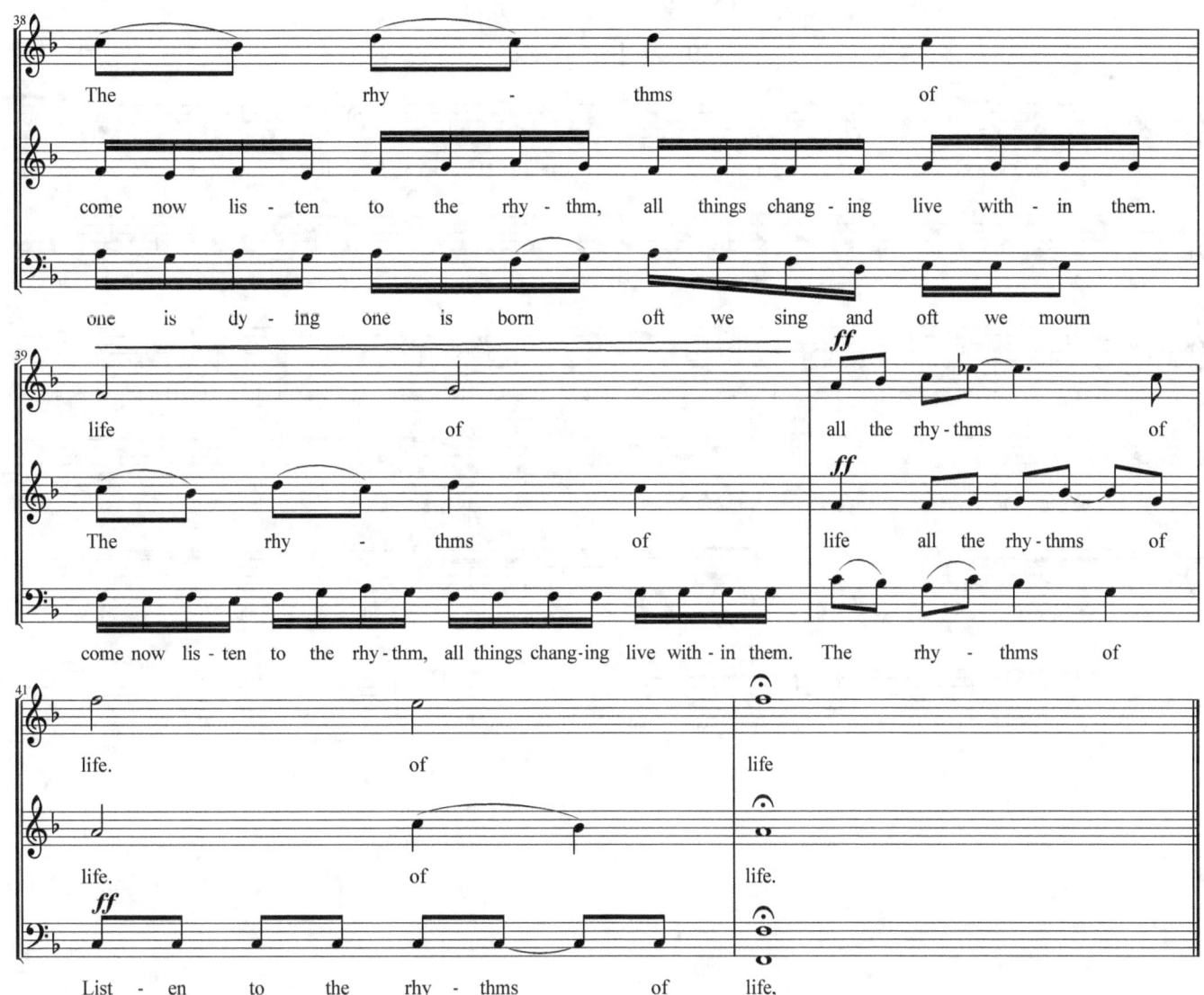

Sing For Joy
(a four part round)

Ken Langer

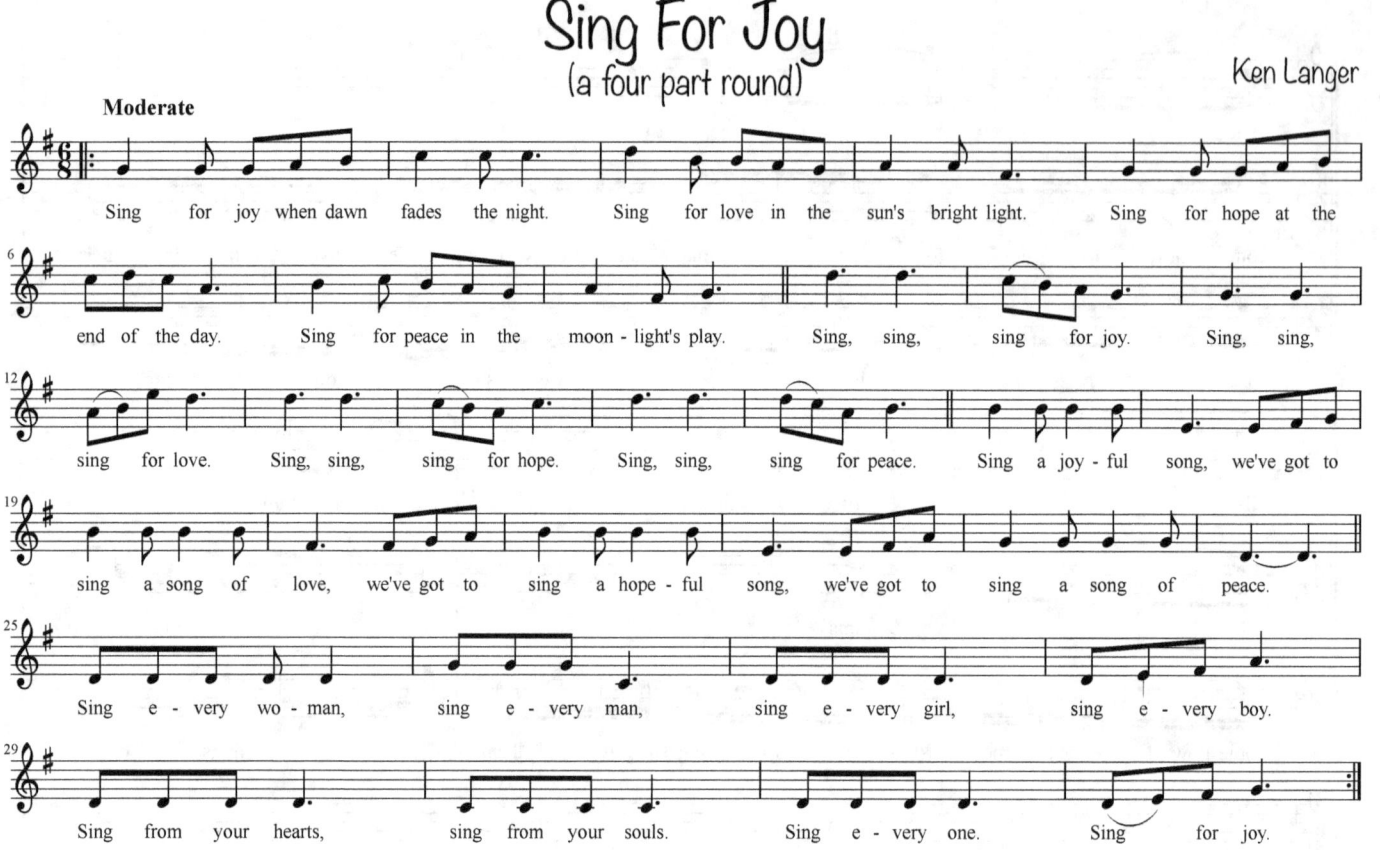

Moderate

Sing for joy when dawn fades the night. Sing for love in the sun's bright light. Sing for hope at the

end of the day. Sing for peace in the moon - light's play. Sing, sing, sing for joy. Sing, sing,

sing for love. Sing, sing, sing for hope. Sing, sing, sing for peace. Sing a joy - ful song, we've got to

sing a song of love, we've got to sing a hope - ful song, we've got to sing a song of peace.

Sing e - very wo - man, sing e - very man, sing e - very girl, sing e - very boy.

Sing from your hearts, sing from your souls. Sing e - very one. Sing for joy.

There's a Presence

(a three part round)

Ken Langer

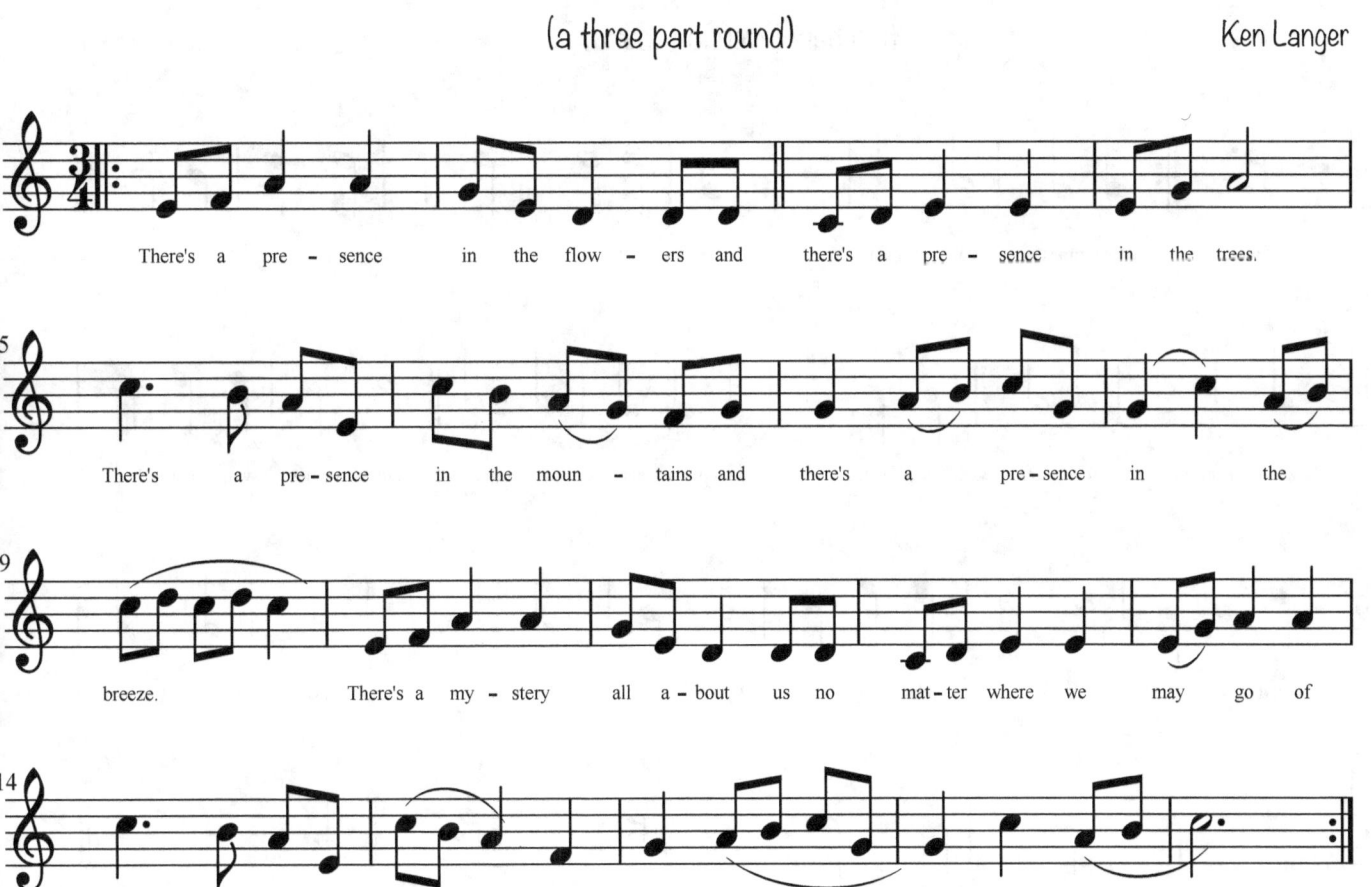

There's a pre - sence in the flow - ers and there's a pre - sence in the trees.

There's a pre - sence in the moun - tains and there's a pre - sence in the

breeze. There's a my - stery all a - bout us no mat - ter where we may go of

which all are a part but few take time to know.

Turn It Around

(a two part inversion round)

Ken Langer

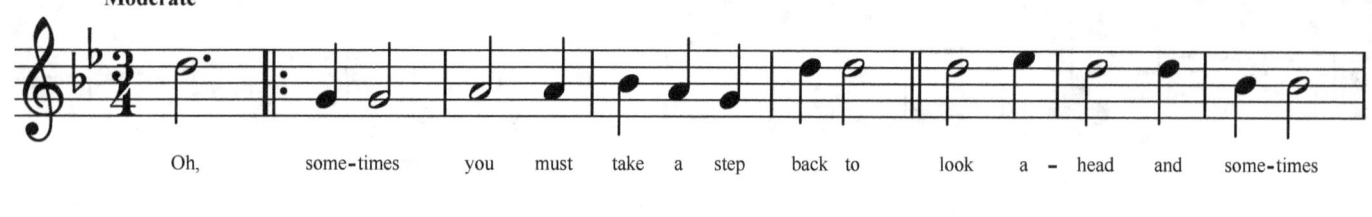

Oh, some-times you must take a step back to look a - head and some-times

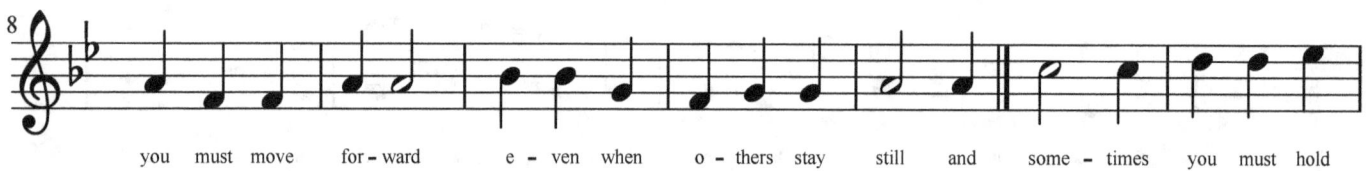

you must move for - ward e - ven when o - thers stay still and some - times you must hold

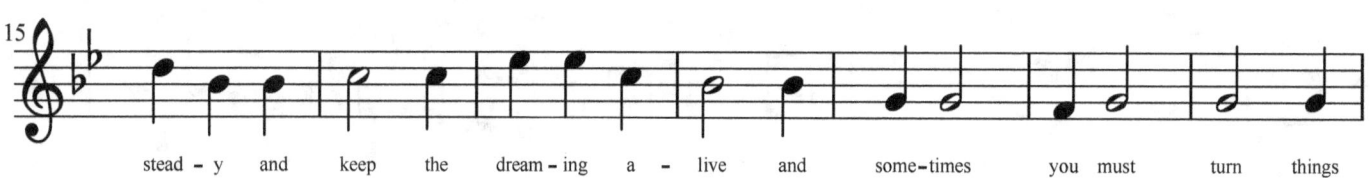

stead - y and keep the dream - ing a - live and some-times you must turn things

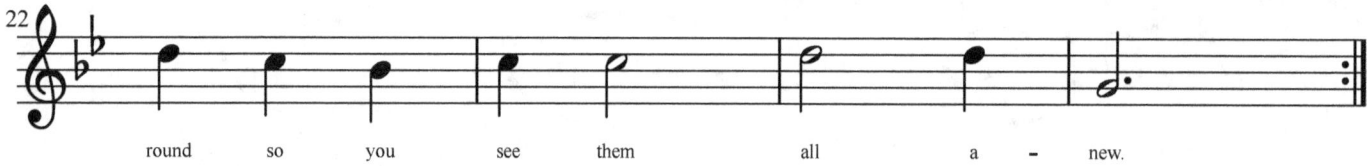

round so you see them all a - new.

Note: The part beginning at the double bar at measure 13 is created by inverting the melody in measures 2- 12.

Seven Hymns

Table Of Contents

Let Us Come Now All Together

Ken Langer

Let us come now all to-ge-ther in heart and mind and
Let us come now all to-ge-ther from pla-ces near and

soul. Let each wor-ship in their own way but seek a com-mon
far. Let us ce-le-brate each o-ther no mat-ter who we

goal: to seek peace in jus-tice and find strength in
are:

love to dance in the spi-rit and sing the song of

1. life. Let us
2. life.

The Growing Light

Samuel Longfellow

Ken Langer

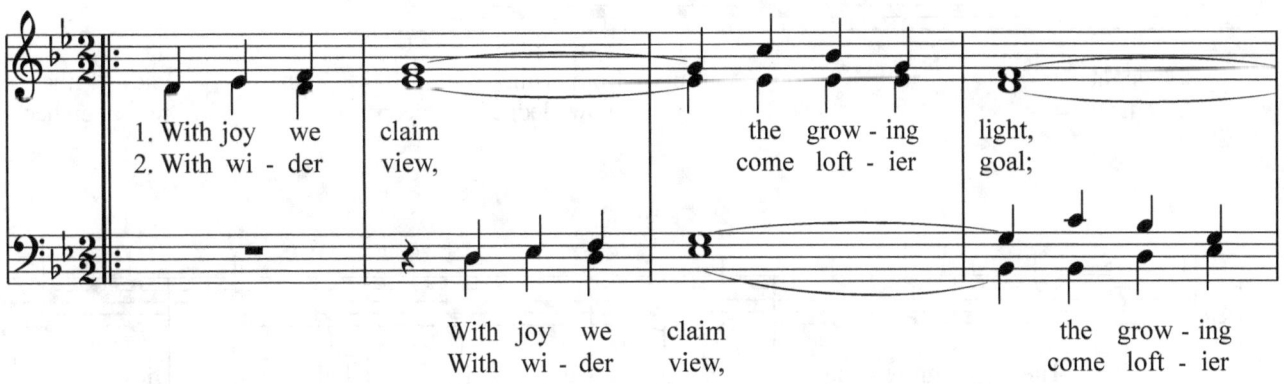

1. With joy we claim the grow - ing light,
2. With wi - der view, come loft - ier goal;

With joy we claim the grow - ing
With wi - der view, come loft - ier

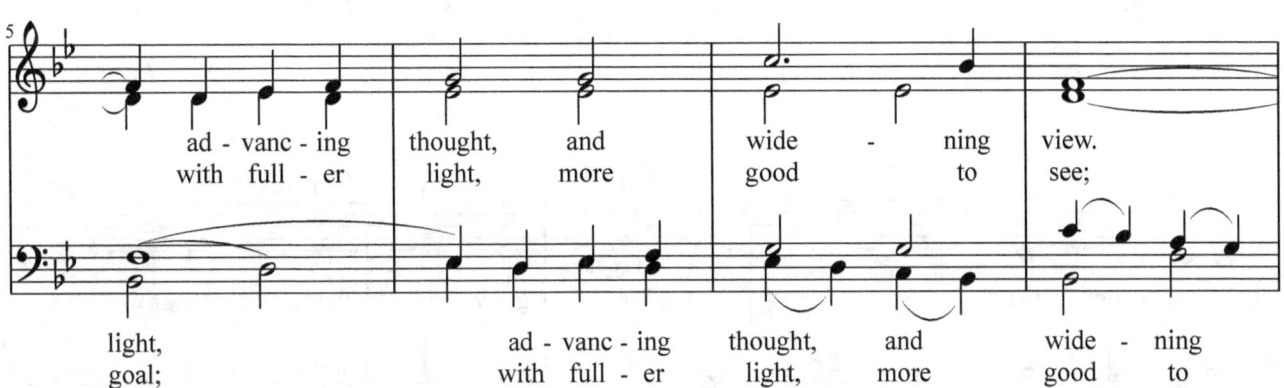

ad - vanc - ing thought, and wide - ning view.
with full - er light, and more good to see;

light, ad - vanc - ing thought, and wide - ning
goal; with full - er light, more good to

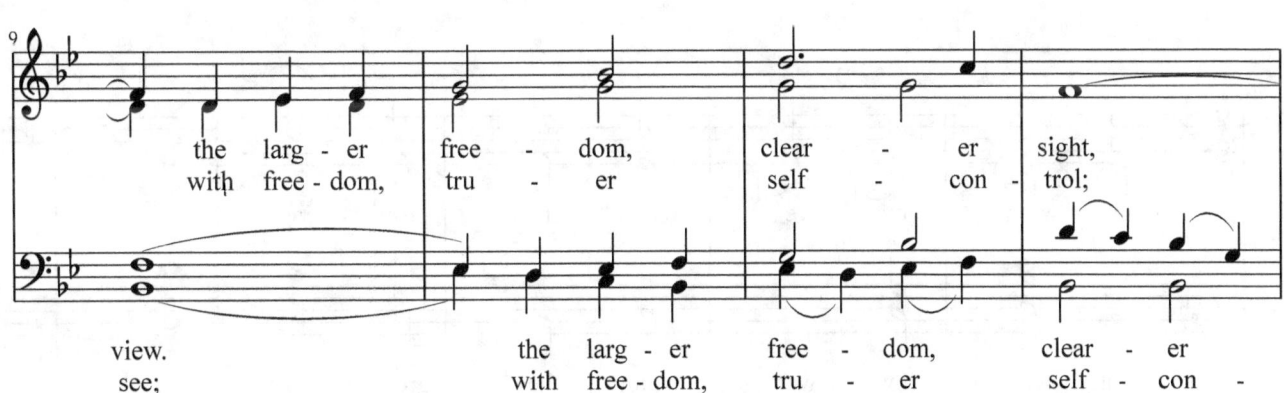

the larg - er free - dom, clear - er sight,
with free - dom, tru - er self - con - trol;

view. the larg - er free - dom, clear - er
see; with free - dom, tru - er self - con -

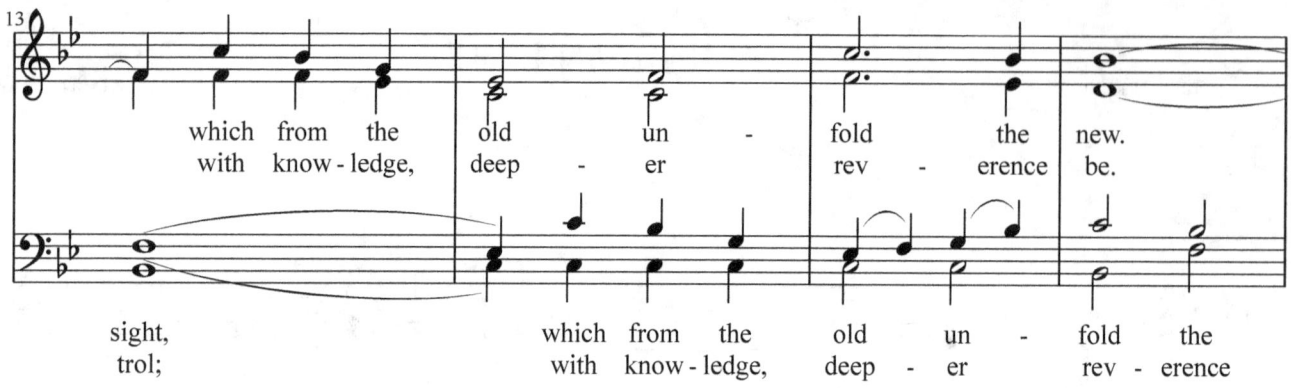

which from the old un - fold the new.
with know - ledge, deep - er rev - erence be.

sight,
trol;
which from the old un - fold the
with know - ledge, deep - er rev - erence

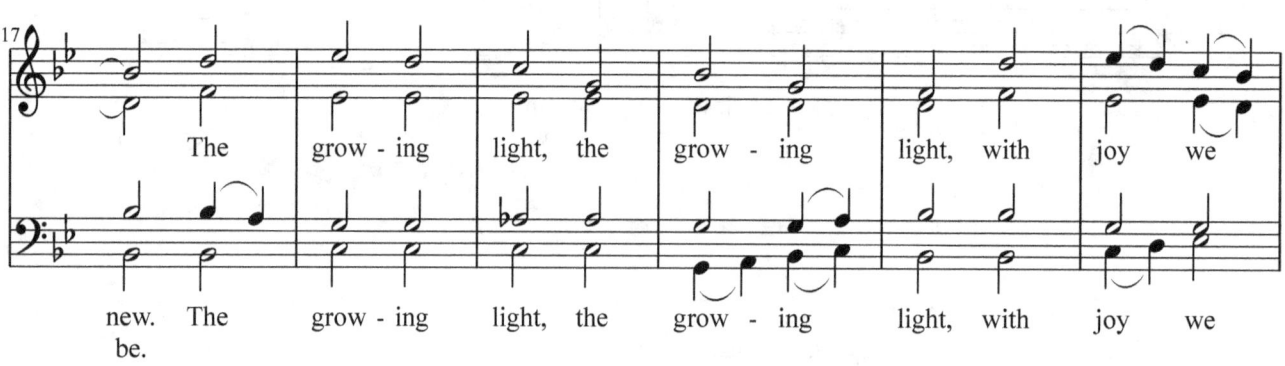

The grow - ing light, the grow - ing light, with joy we

new. The grow - ing light, the grow - ing light, with joy we
be.

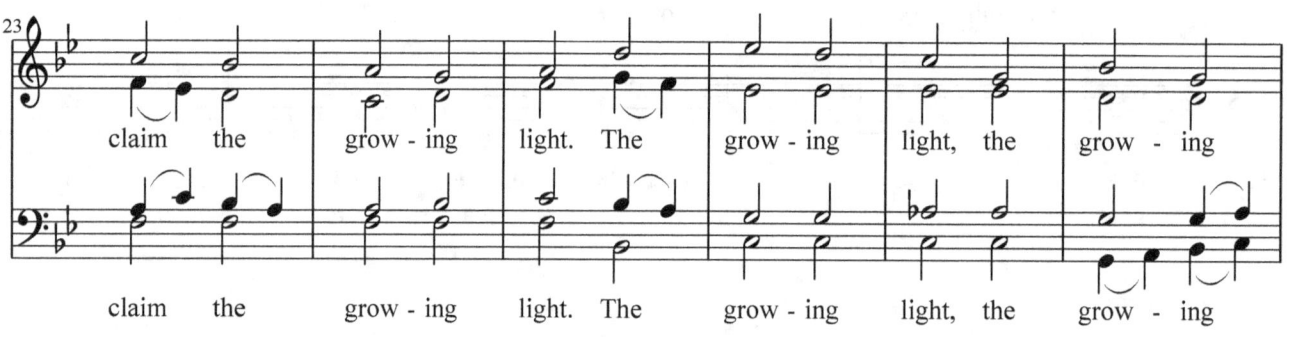

claim the grow - ing light. The grow - ing light, the grow - ing

claim the grow - ing light. The grow - ing light, the grow - ing

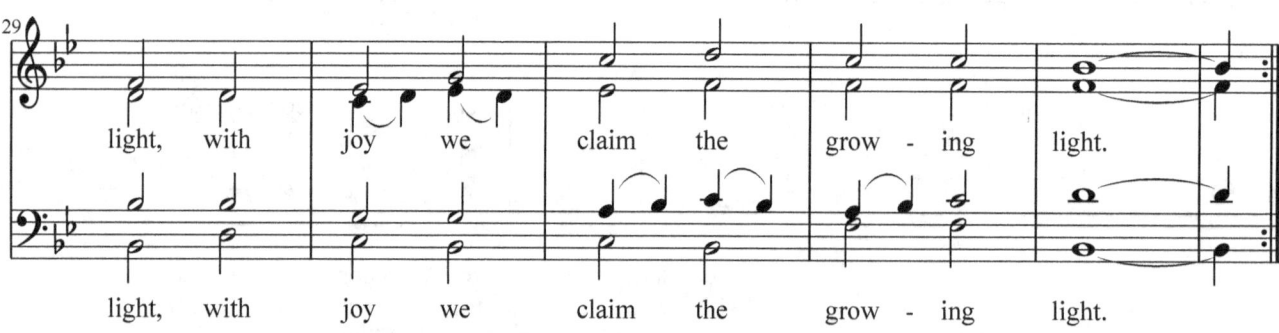

light, with joy we claim the grow - ing light.

light, with joy we claim the grow - ing light.

Immortal Love

John Whittier

Ken Langer

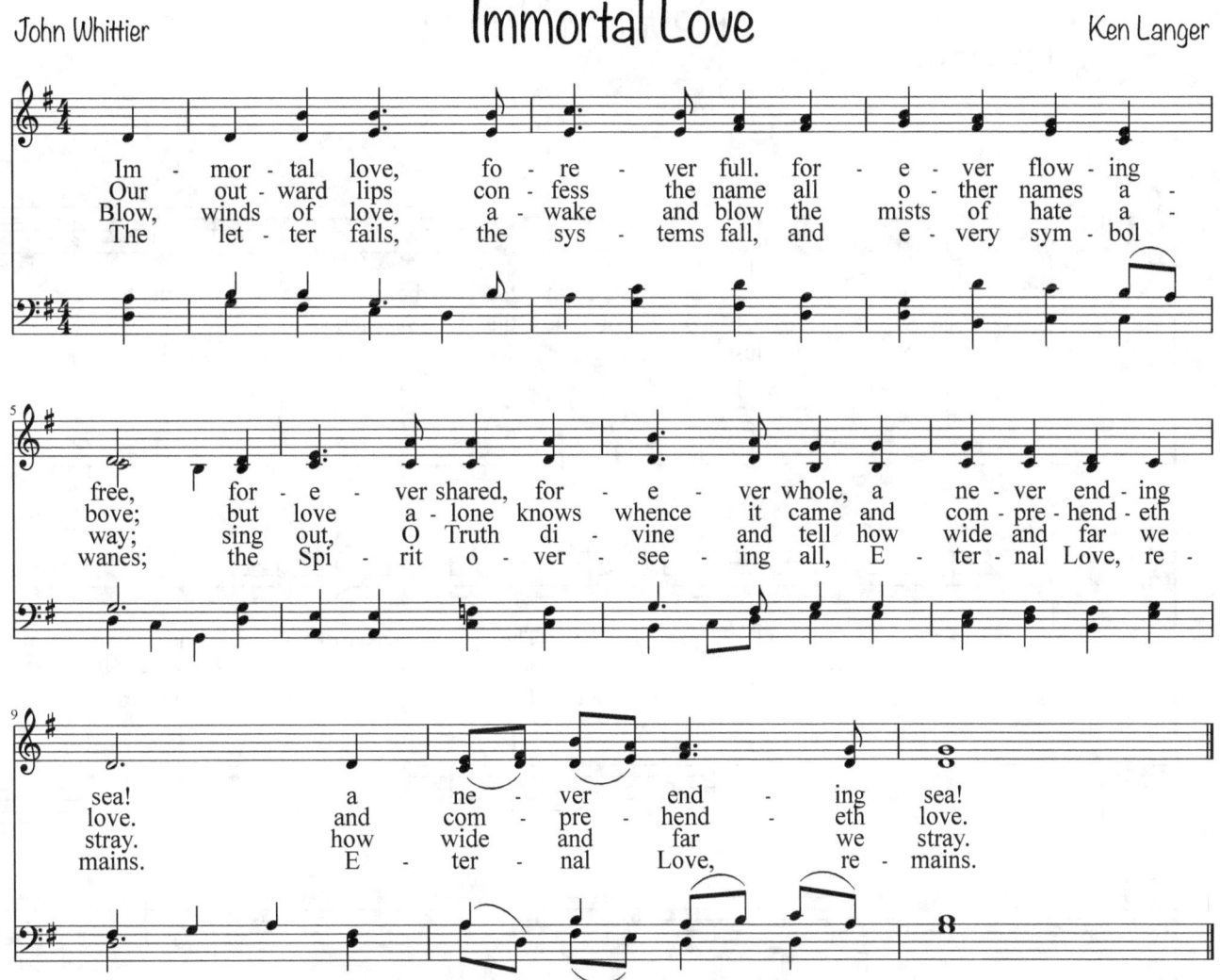

Im - mor - tal love, fo - re - ver full. for - e - ver flow - ing
Our out - ward lips con - fess the name all o - ther names a -
Blow, winds of love, a - wake and blow the mists of hate a -
The let - ter fails, the sys - tems fall, and e - very sym - bol

free, for - e - ver shared, for - e - ver whole, a ne - ver end - ing
bove; but love a - lone knows whence it came and com - pre - hend - eth
way; sing out, O Truth di - vine and tell how wide and far we
wanes; the Spi - rit o - ver - see - ing all, E - ter - nal Love, re -

sea! a ne - ver end - ing sea!
love. and com - pre - hend - eth love.
stray. how wide and far we stray.
mains. E - ter - nal Love, re - mains.

Revealed In Us

taken from R.W. Emerson

Ken Langer

Fast (waltz-like)

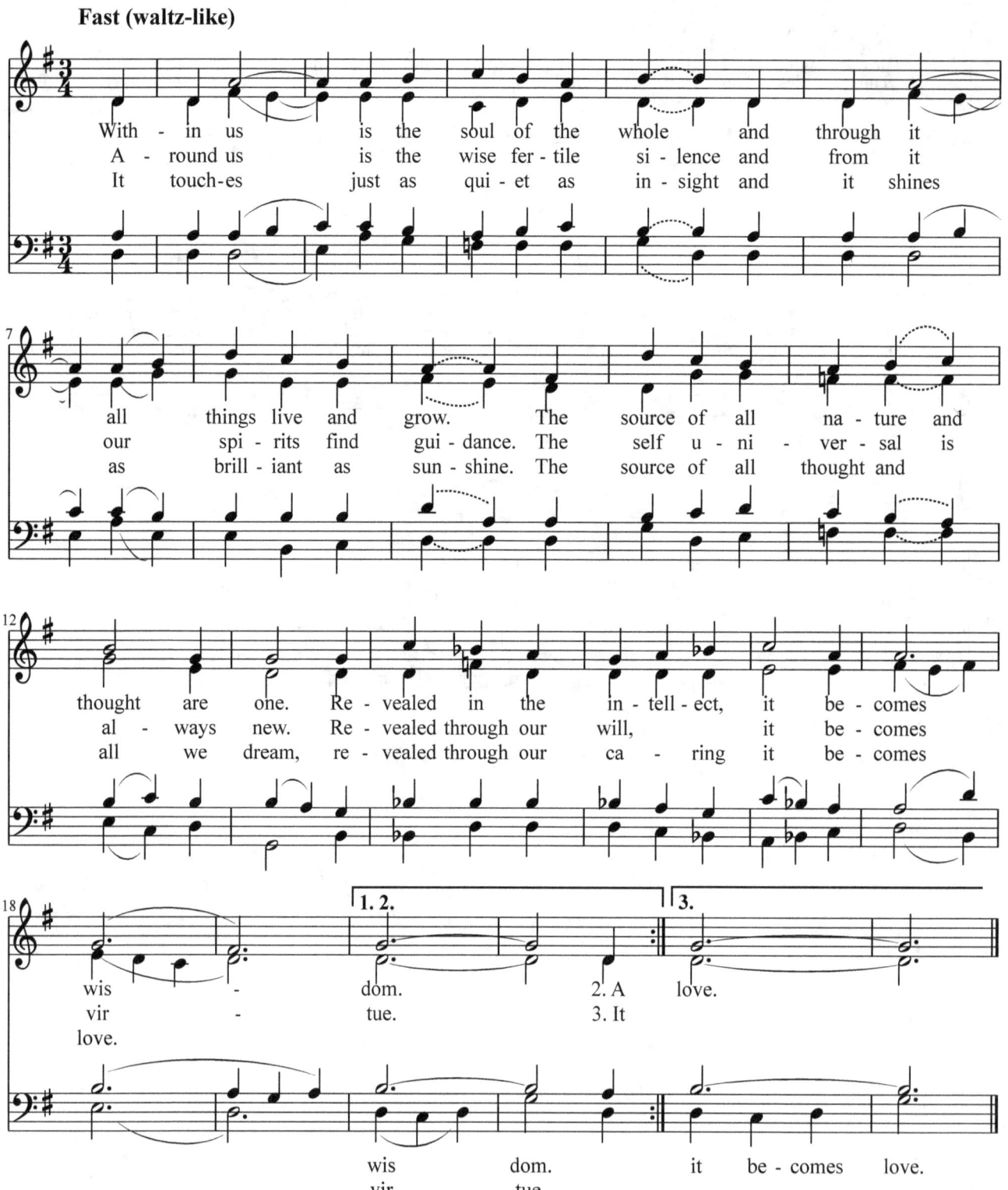

With - in us is the soul of the whole and through it
A - round us is the wise fer - tile si - lence and from it
It touch-es just as qui-et as in - sight and it shines

all things live and grow. The source of all na - ture and
our spi - rits find gui - dance. The self u - ni - ver - sal is
as brill - iant as sun - shine. The source of all thought and

thought are one. Re - vealed in the in - tell - ect, it be - comes
al - ways new. Re - vealed through our will, it be - comes
all we dream, re - vealed through our ca - ring it be - comes

1. 2.

3.

wis - dom.   2. A love.
vir - tue.   3. It
love.

wis dom.   it be - comes love.
vir tue.

Sacred Space

Ken Langer

1. In the space be - tween the mea - sures where the notes in turn are born, si - lence

2. In the space be - tween the stit - ches where the fab - ric finds its form,

is the mu-sic's cra - dle; lift your voice to praise or mourn. As we sing our song to-

geth - er we cre - ate a sac-red space. Ho-ly is the space be - tween us; may our song be an em - brace.

That Great and Fiery Force

Hildegard of Bingen

Ken Langer

Moderate

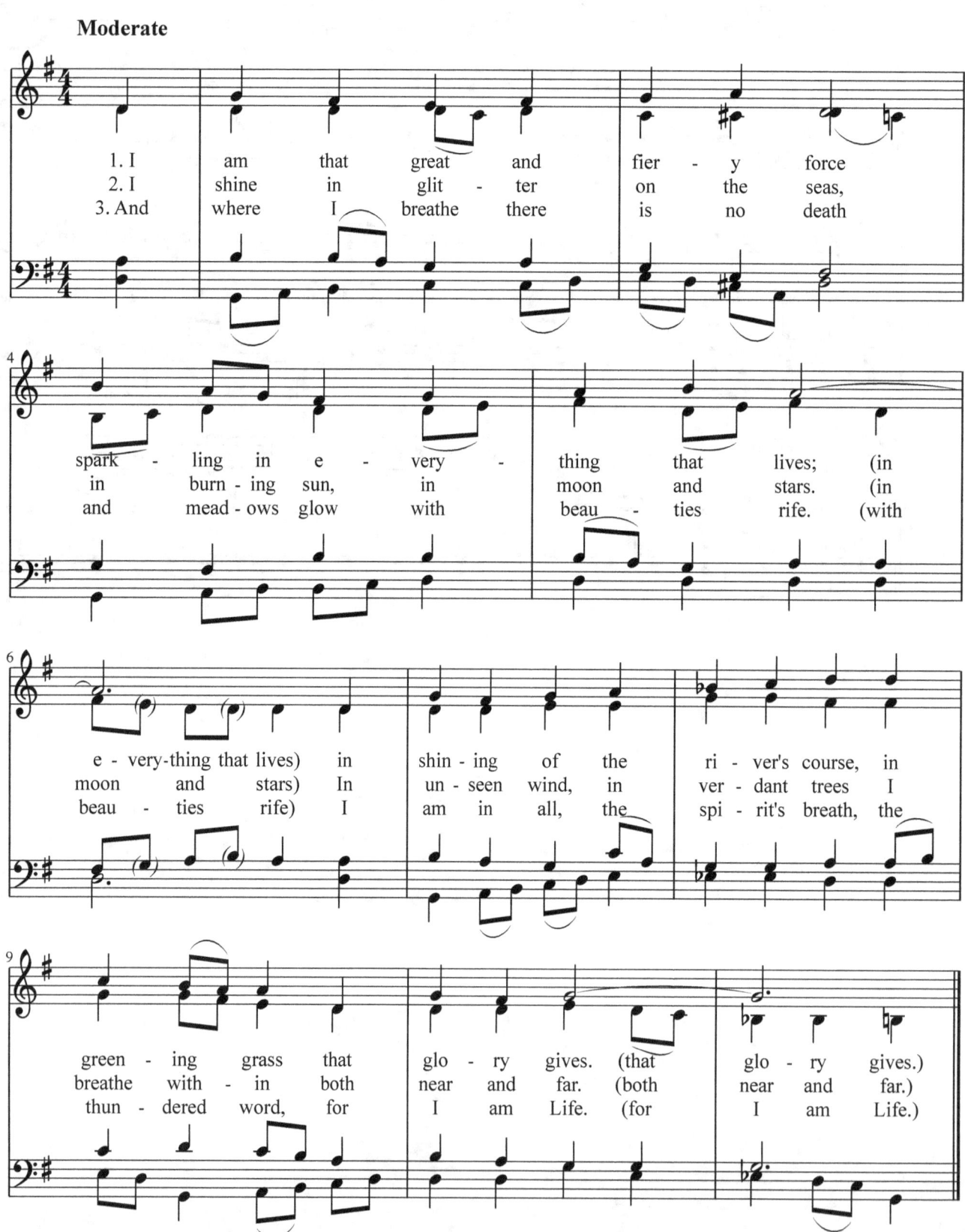

1. I am that great and fier - y force spark - ling in e - very - thing that lives; (in e - very-thing that lives) in shin - ing of the ri - ver's course, in green - ing grass that glo - ry gives. (that glo - ry gives.)

2. I shine in glit - ter on the seas, in burn - ing sun, in moon and stars. (in moon and stars) In un - seen wind, in ver - dant trees I breathe with - in both near and far. (both near and far.)

3. And where I breathe there is no death and mead - ows glow with beau - ties rife. (with beau - ties rife) I am in all, the spi - rit's breath, the thun - dered word, for I am Life. (for I am Life.)

We Are All Sacred

Ken Langer

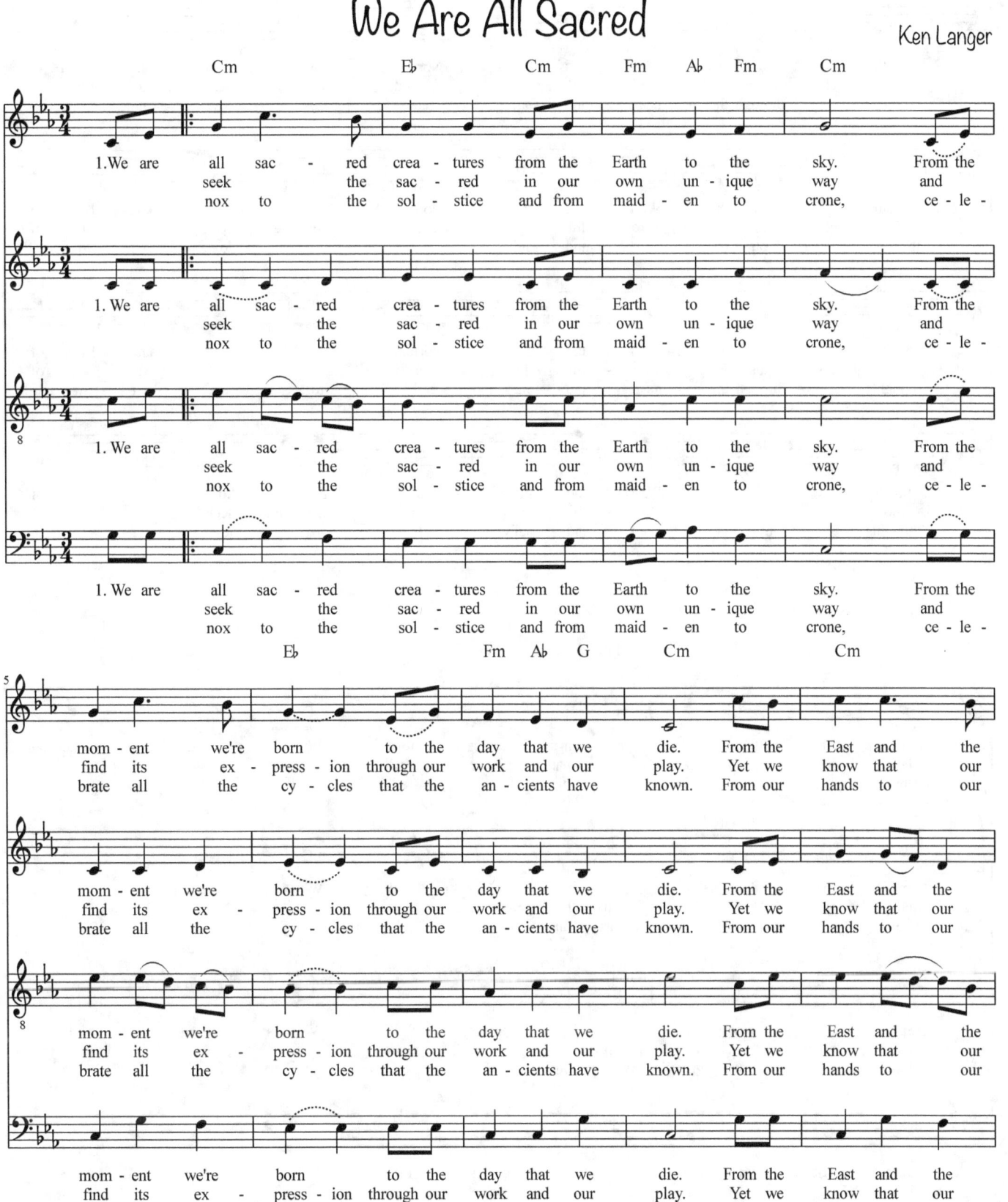

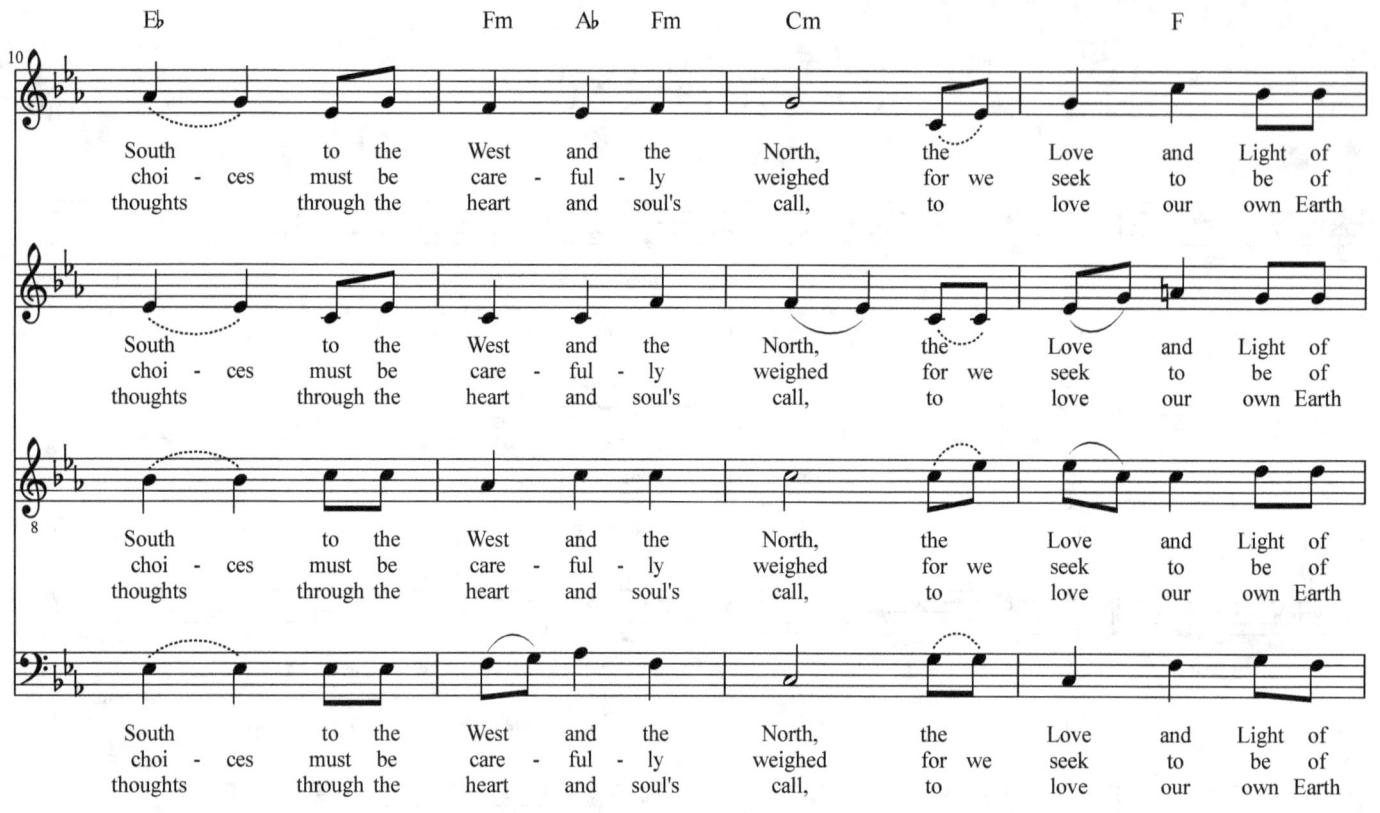

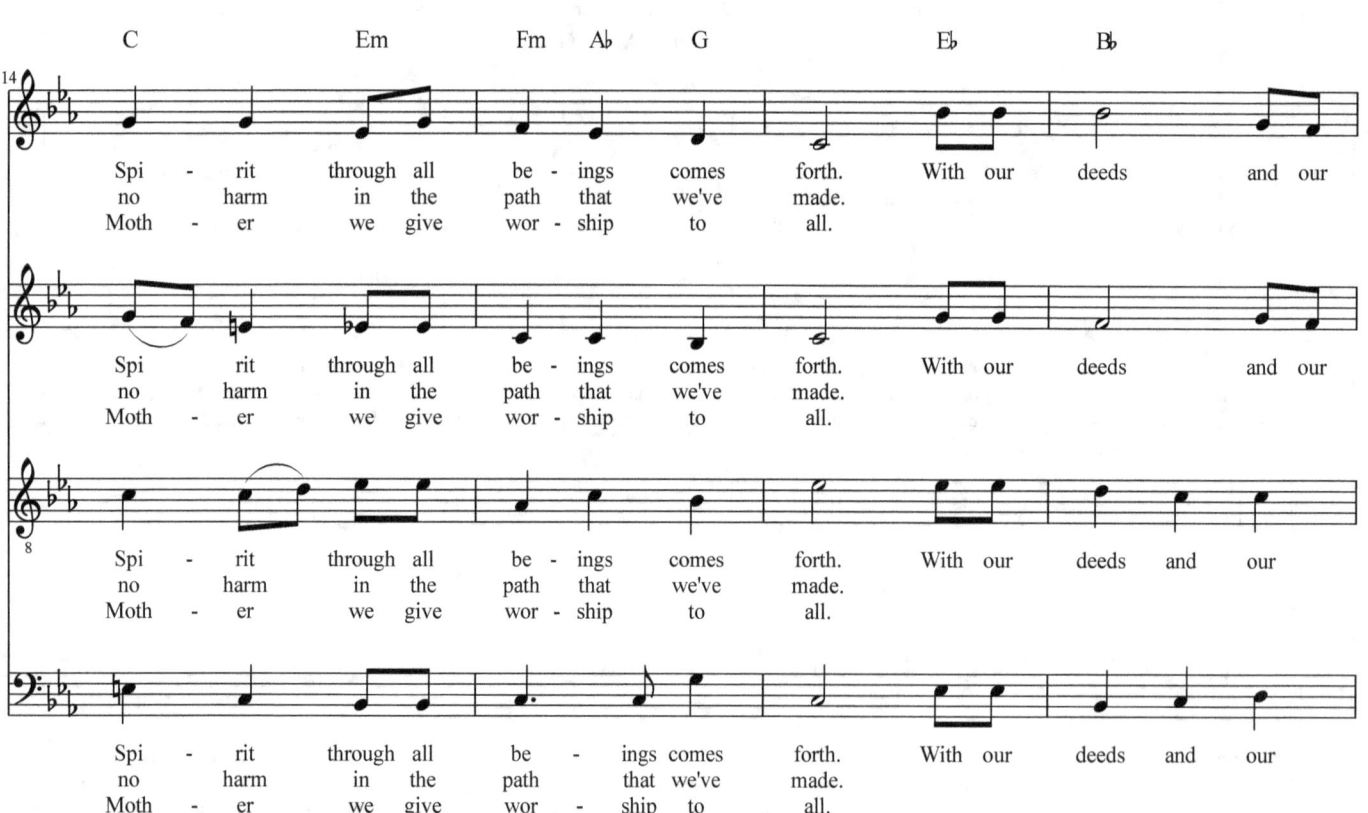

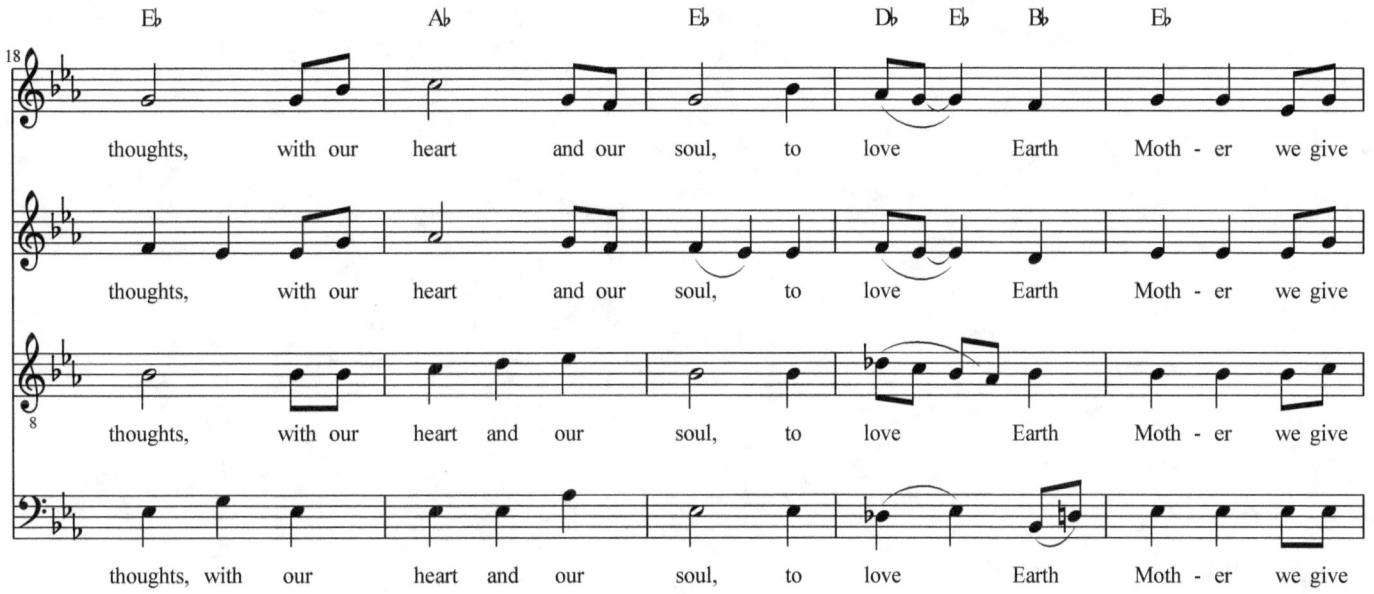

thoughts, with our heart and our soul, to love Earth Moth - er we give

thoughts, with our heart and our soul, to love Earth Moth - er we give

thoughts, with our heart and our soul, to love Earth Moth - er we give

thoughts, with our heart and our soul, to love Earth Moth - er we give

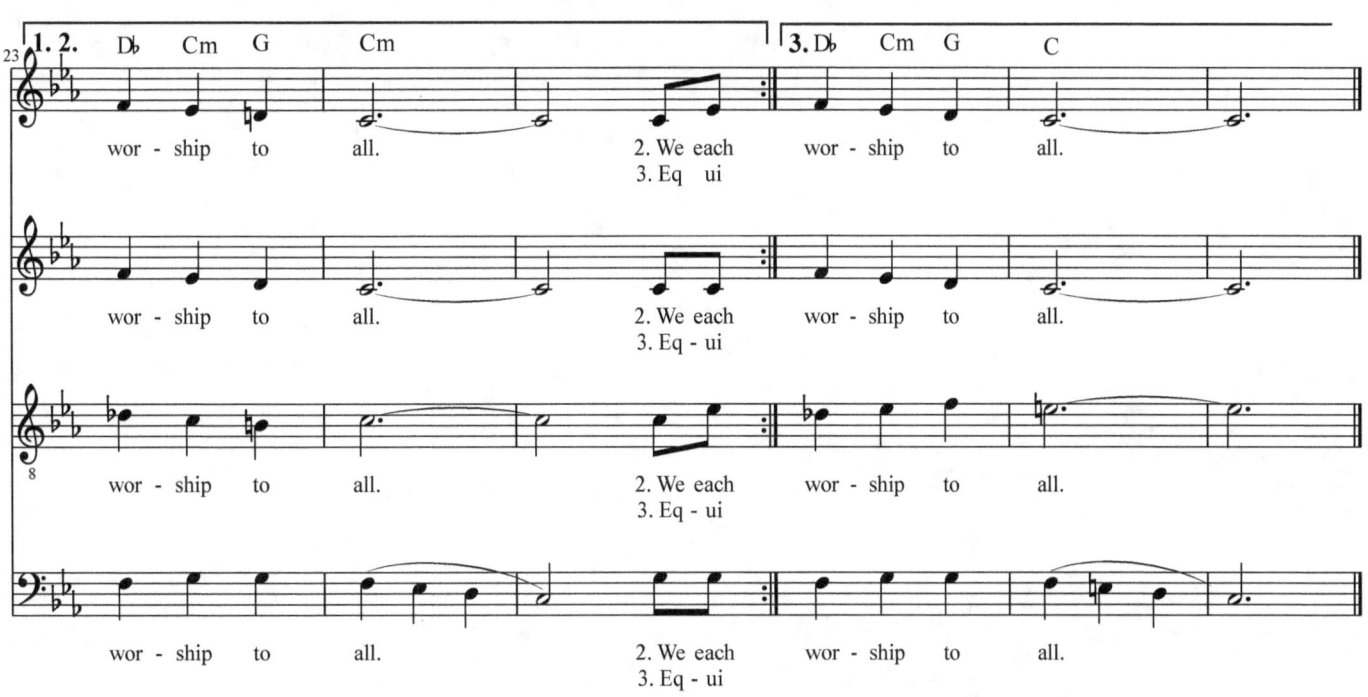

wor - ship to all. 2. We each wor - ship to all.
3. Eq - ui

wor - ship to all. 2. We each wor - ship to all.
3. Eq - ui

wor - ship to all. 2. We each wor - ship to all.
3. Eq - ui

wor - ship to all. 2. We each wor - ship to all.
3. Eq - ui

Three Songs of Rain

Ken Langer

I. When I See Rain

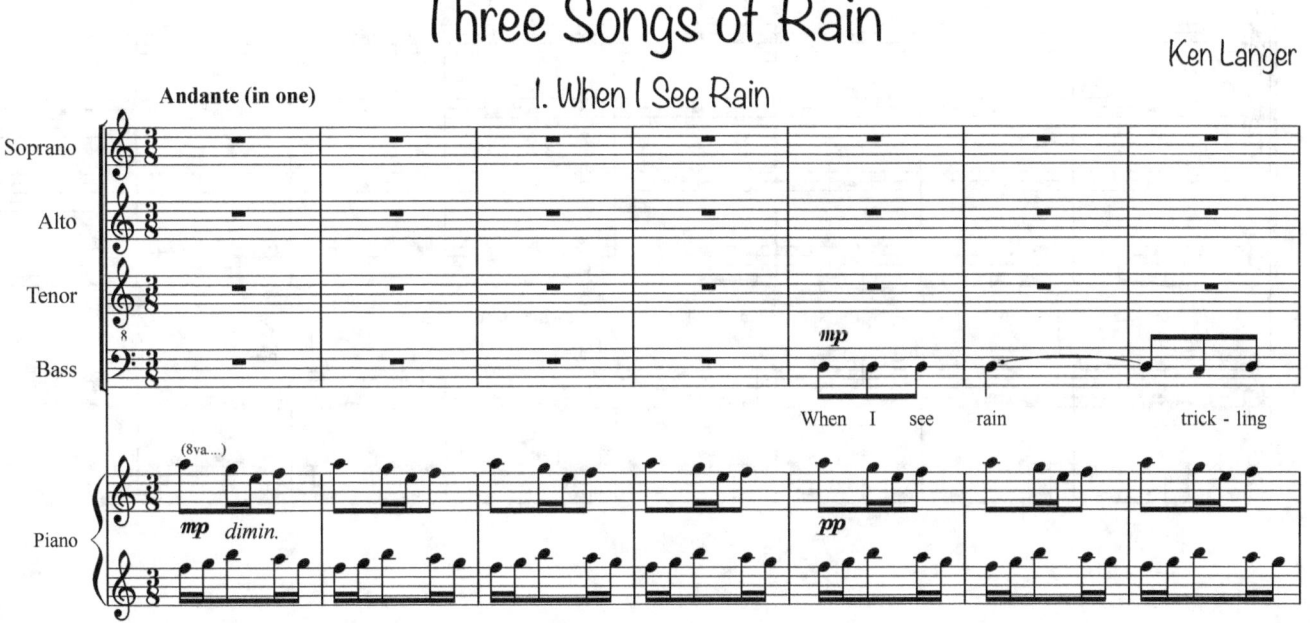

When I see rain trick - ling

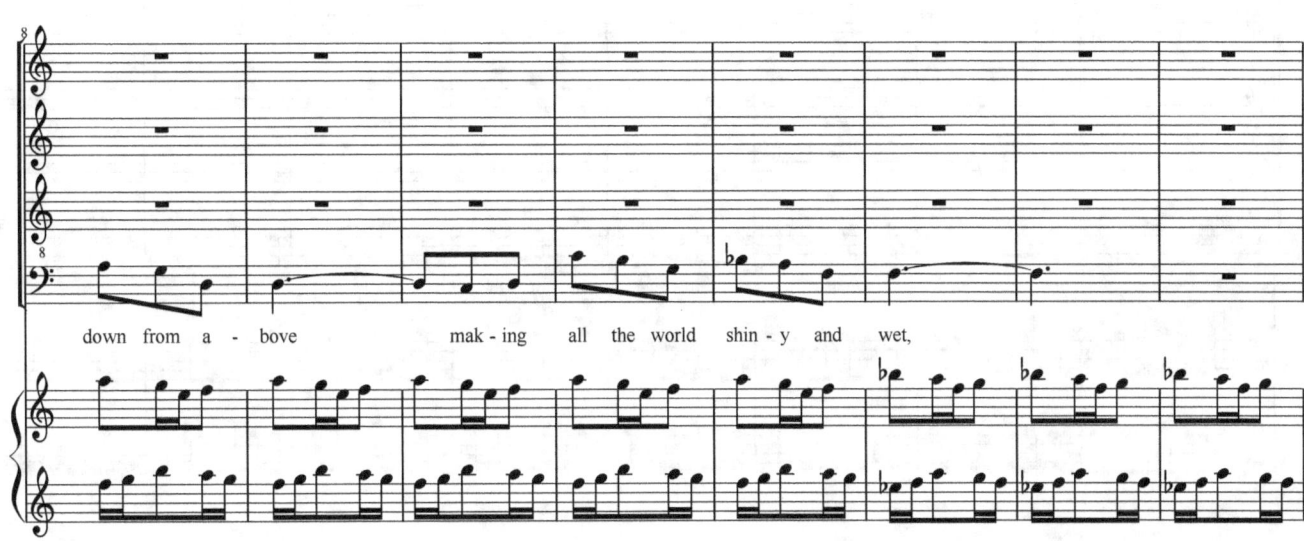

down from a - bove mak - ing all the world shin - y and wet,

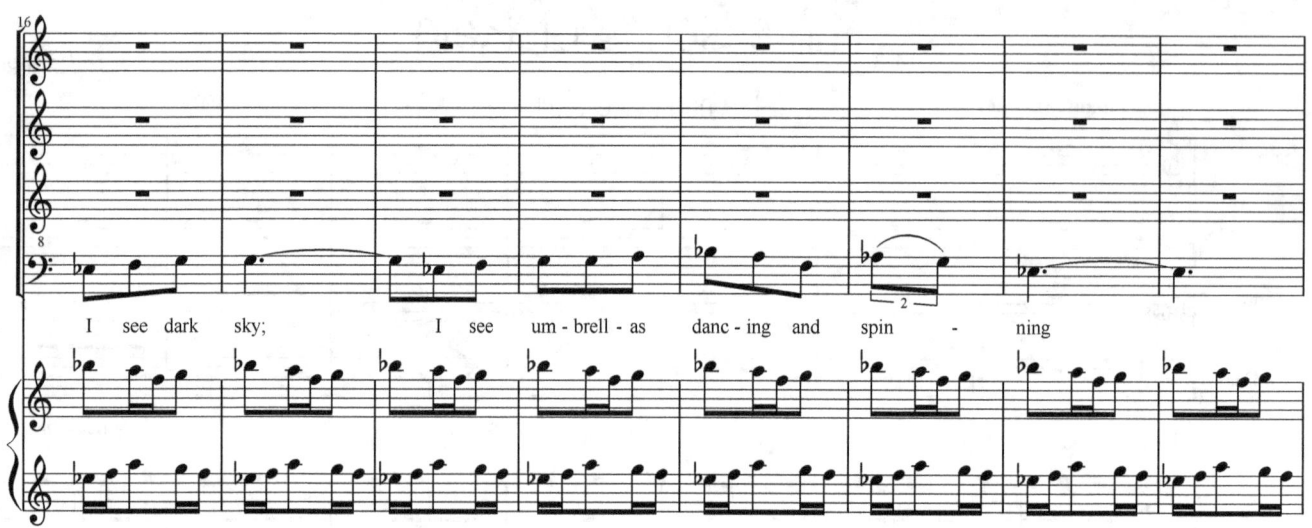

I see dark sky;   I see um - brell - as   danc - ing   and   spin - ning

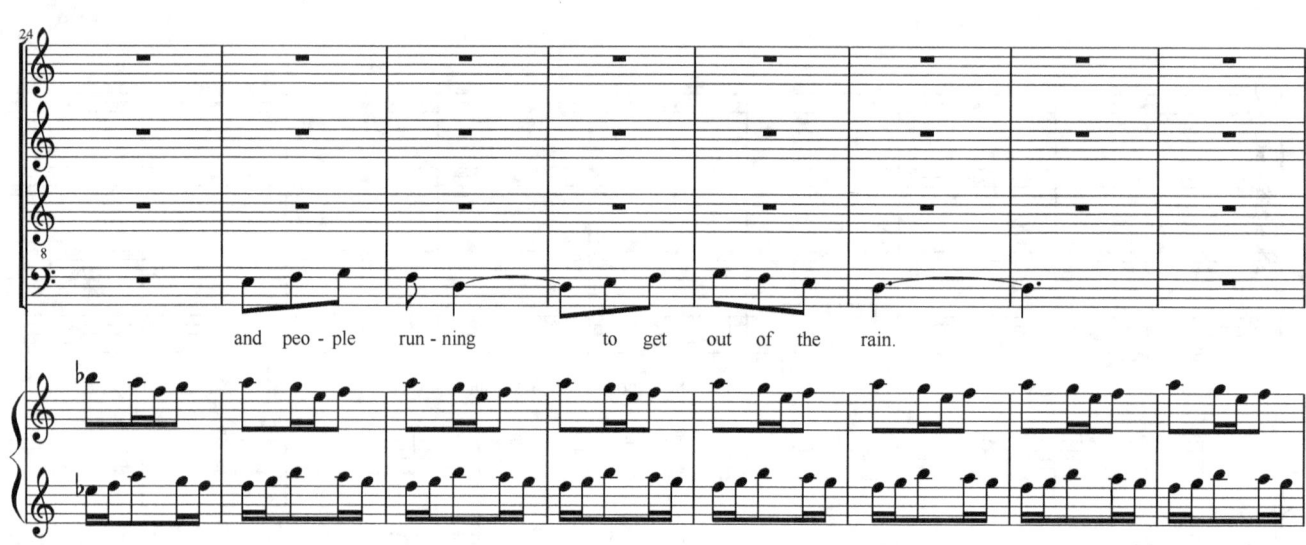

and   peo - ple   run - ning   to   get   out   of   the   rain.

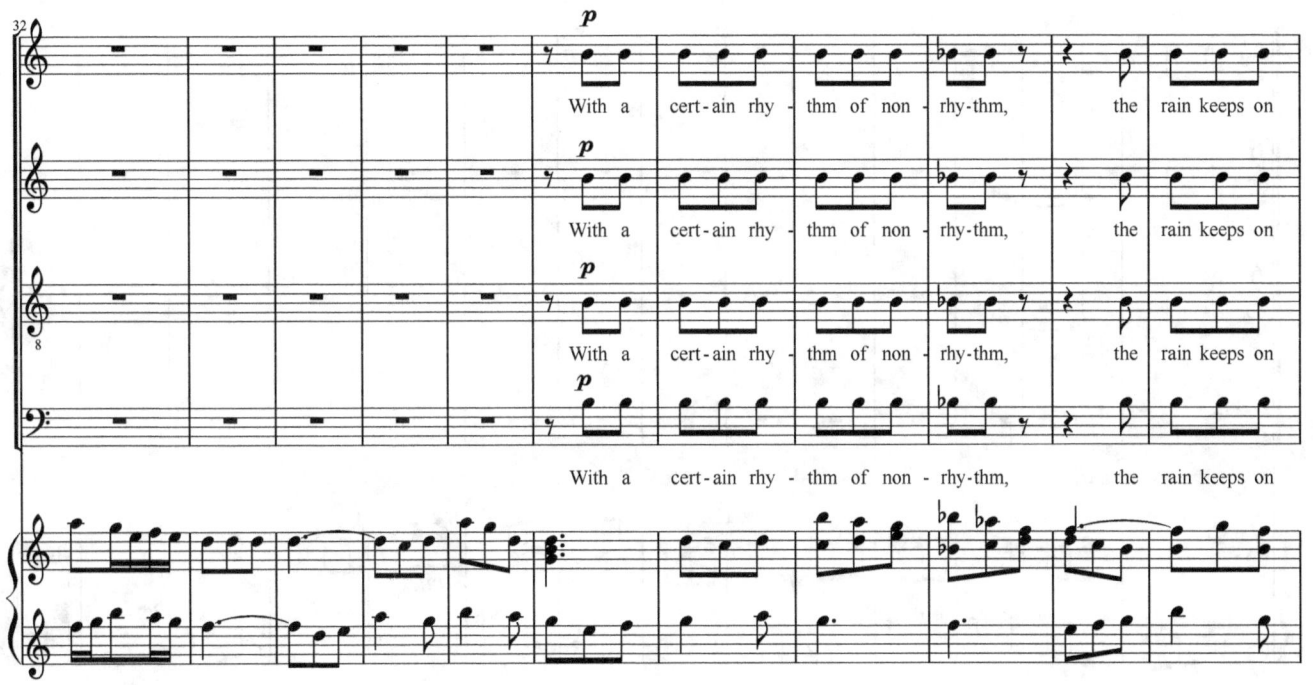

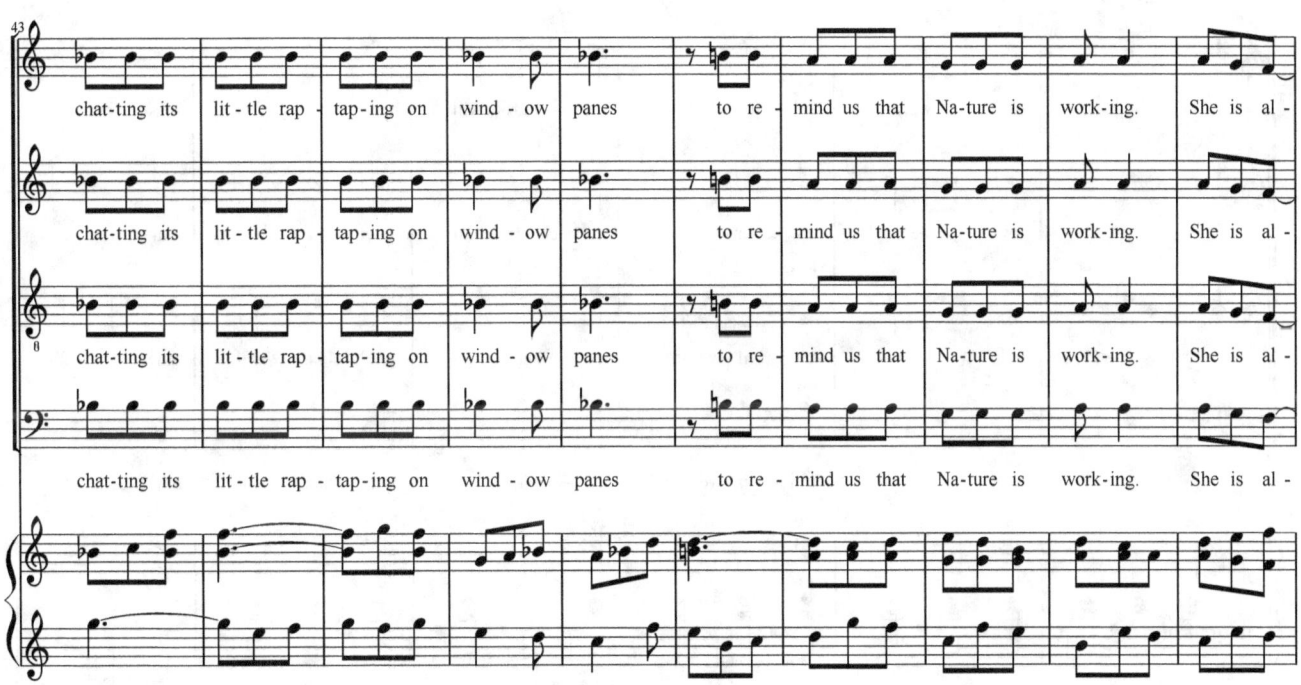

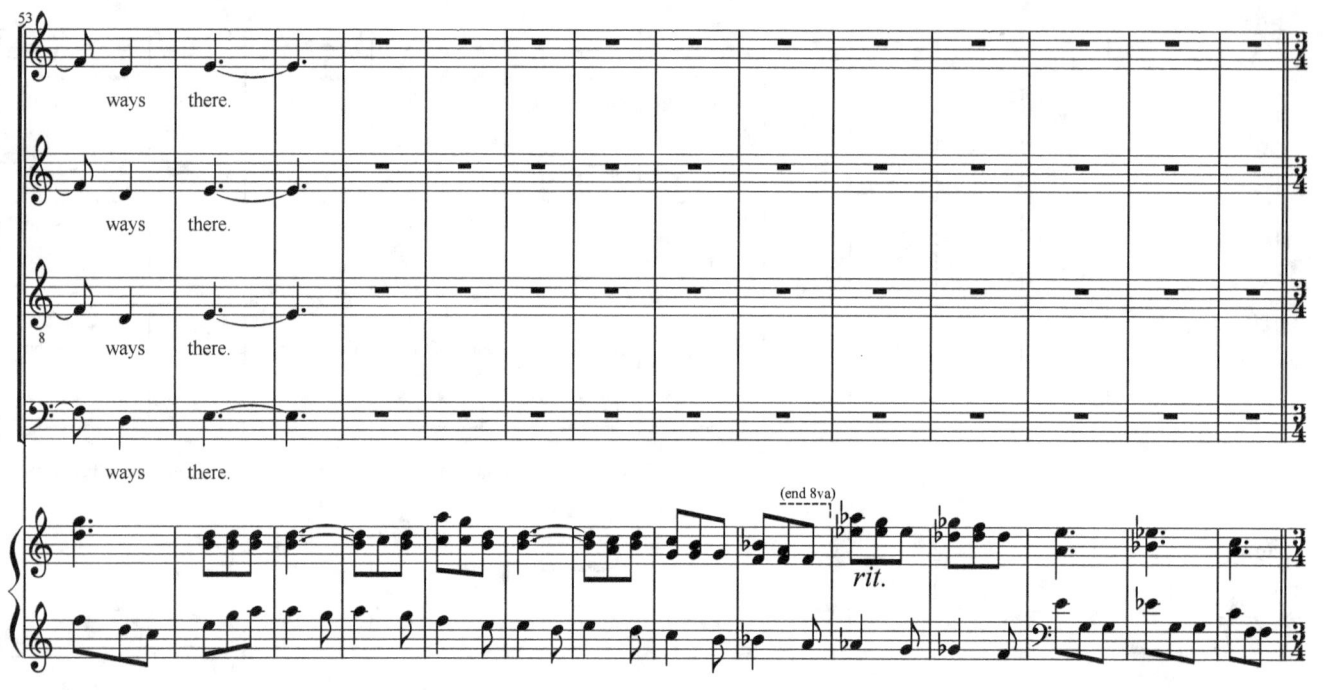

Adagio

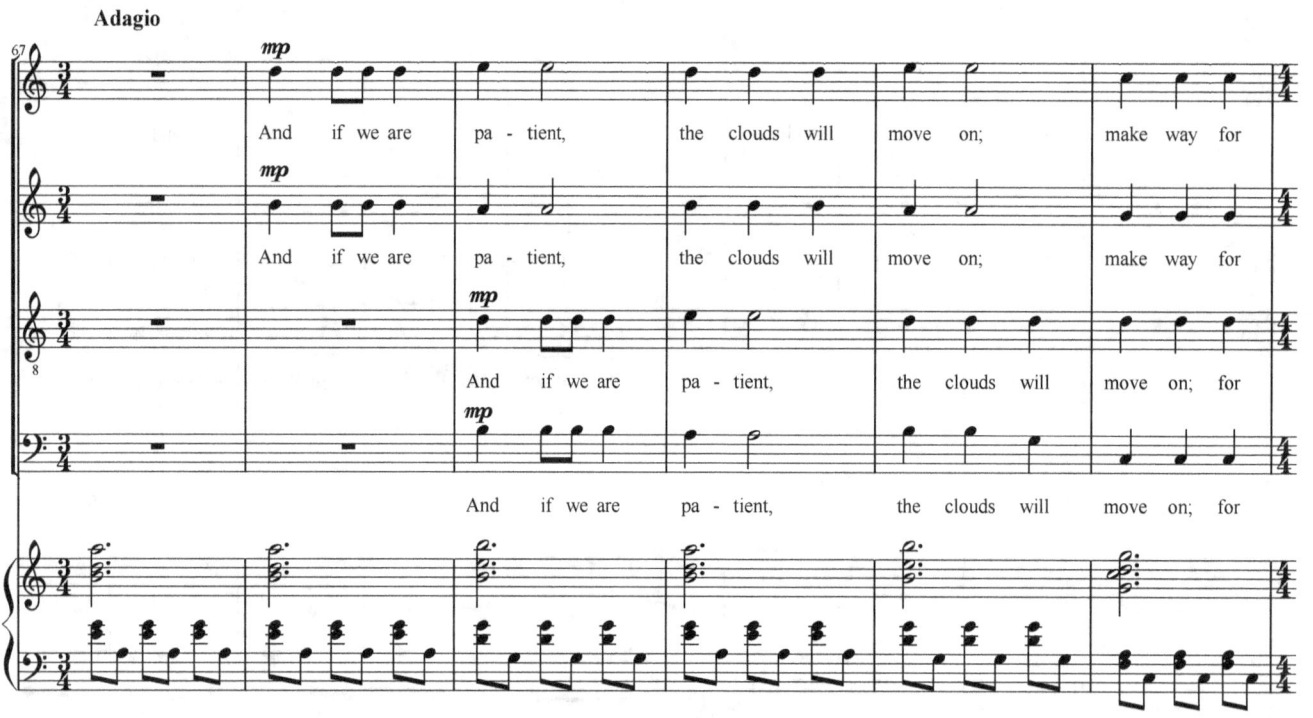

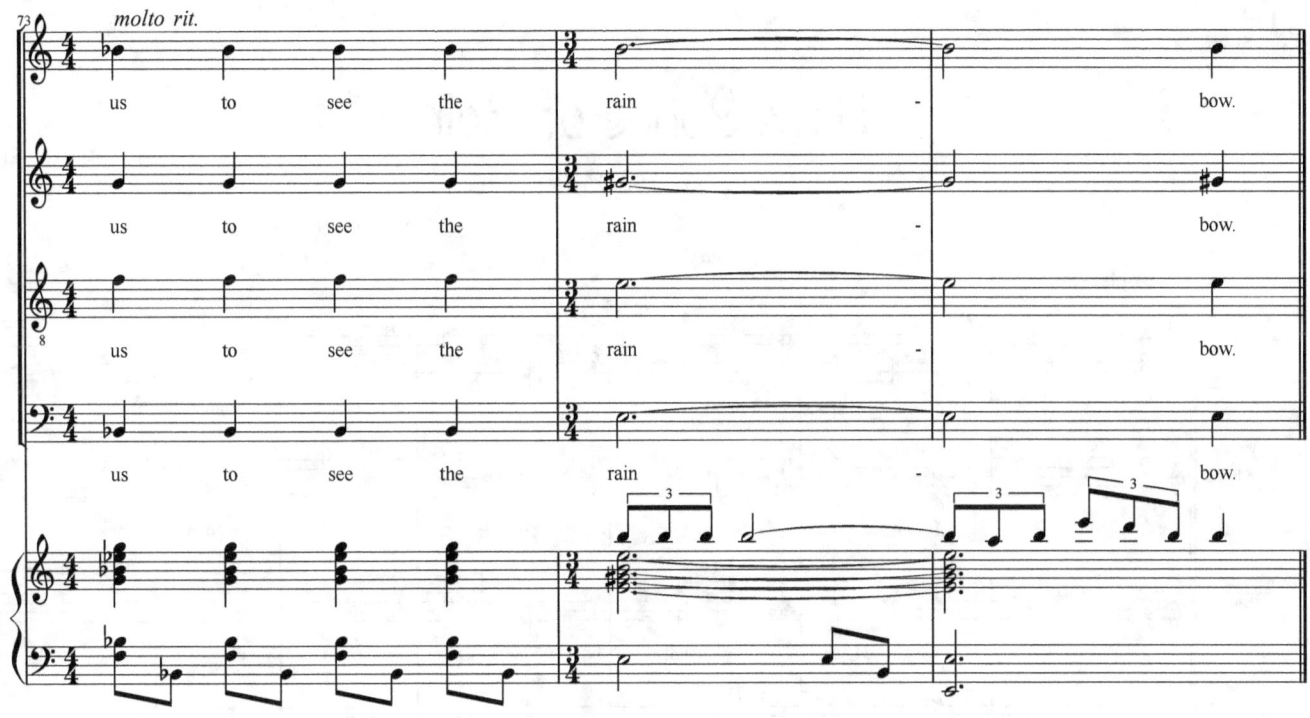

Three Songs of Rain

2. As You Left

Ken Langer

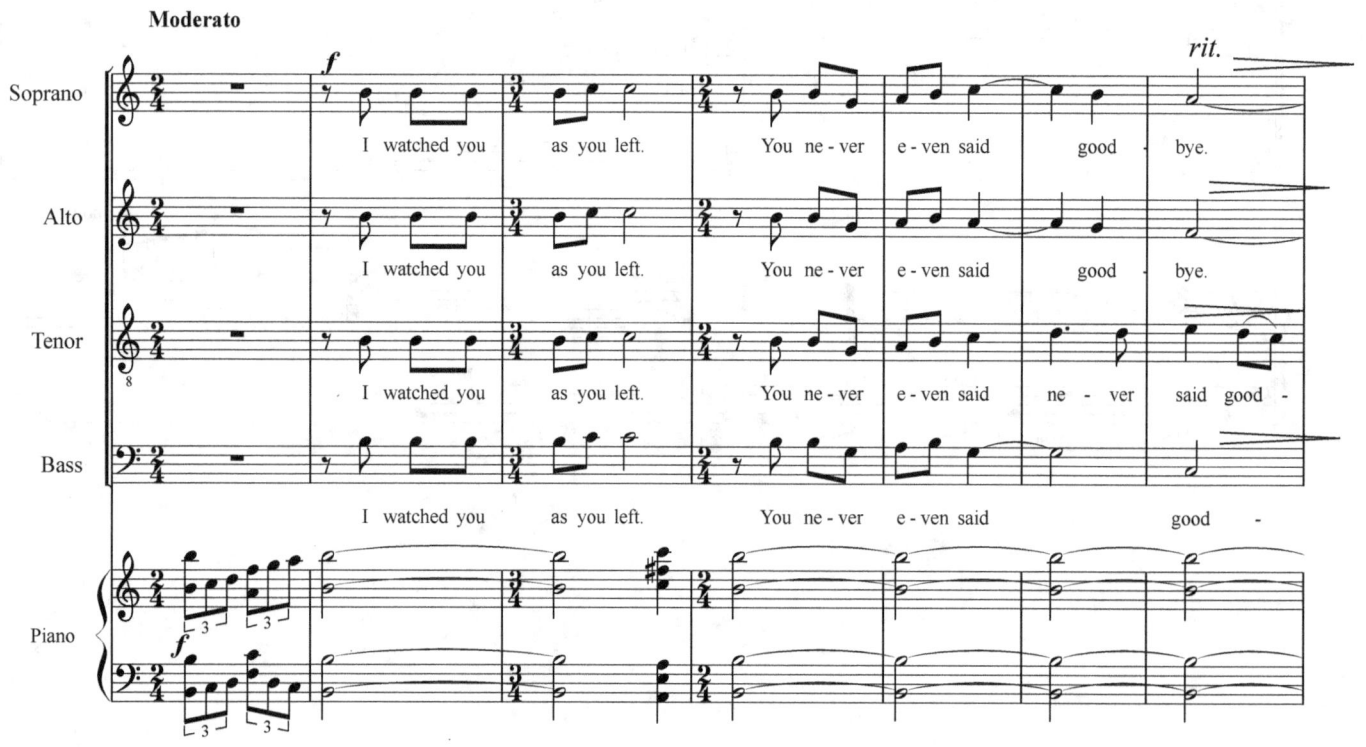

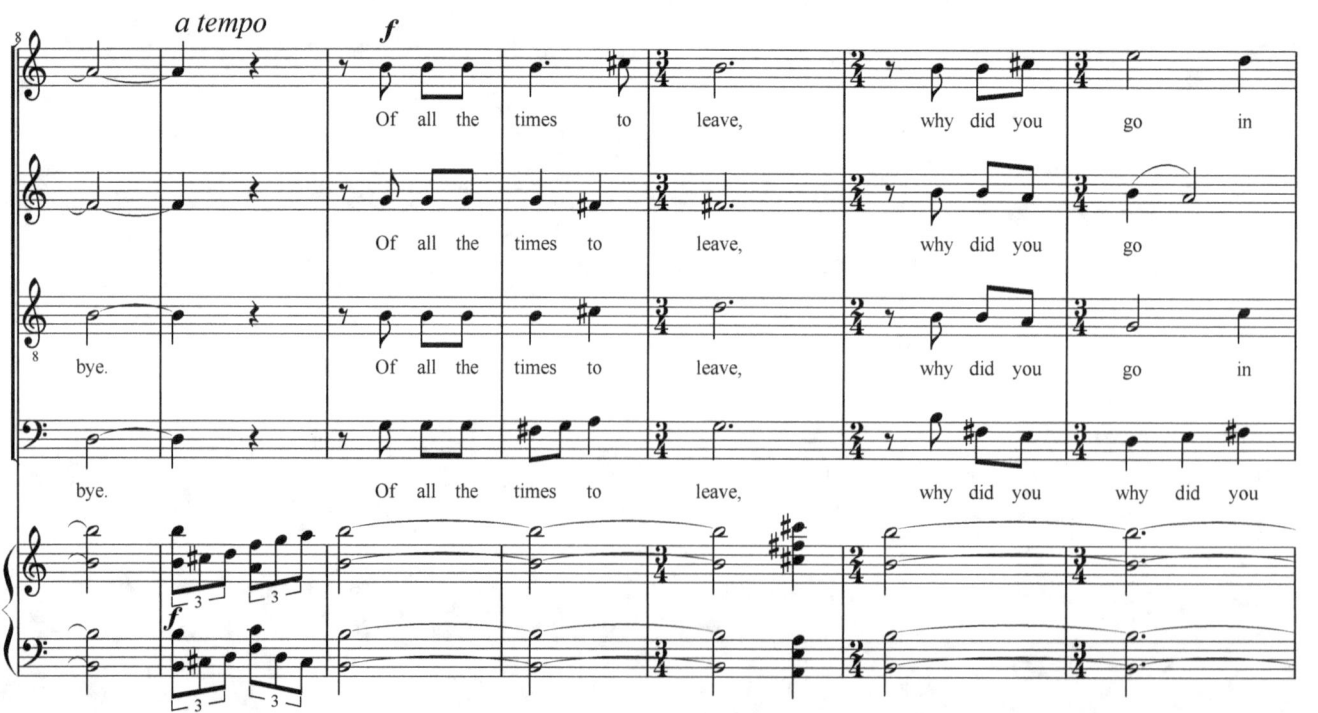

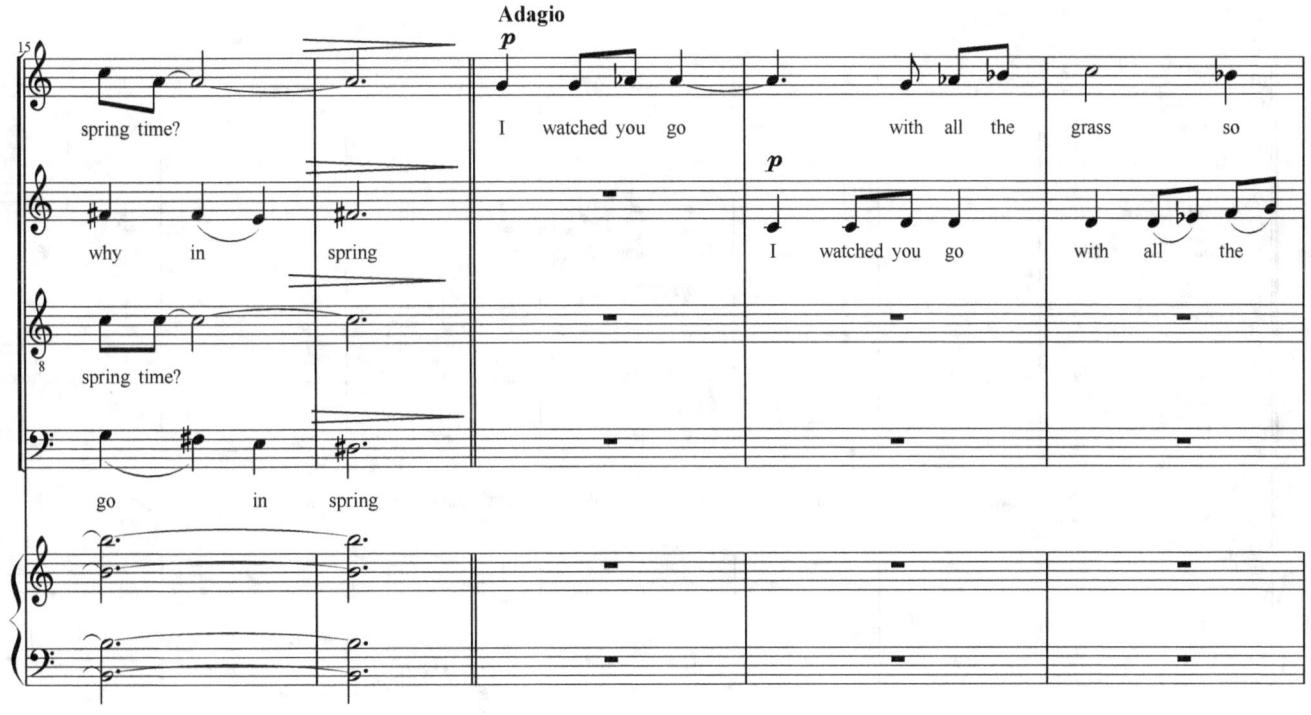

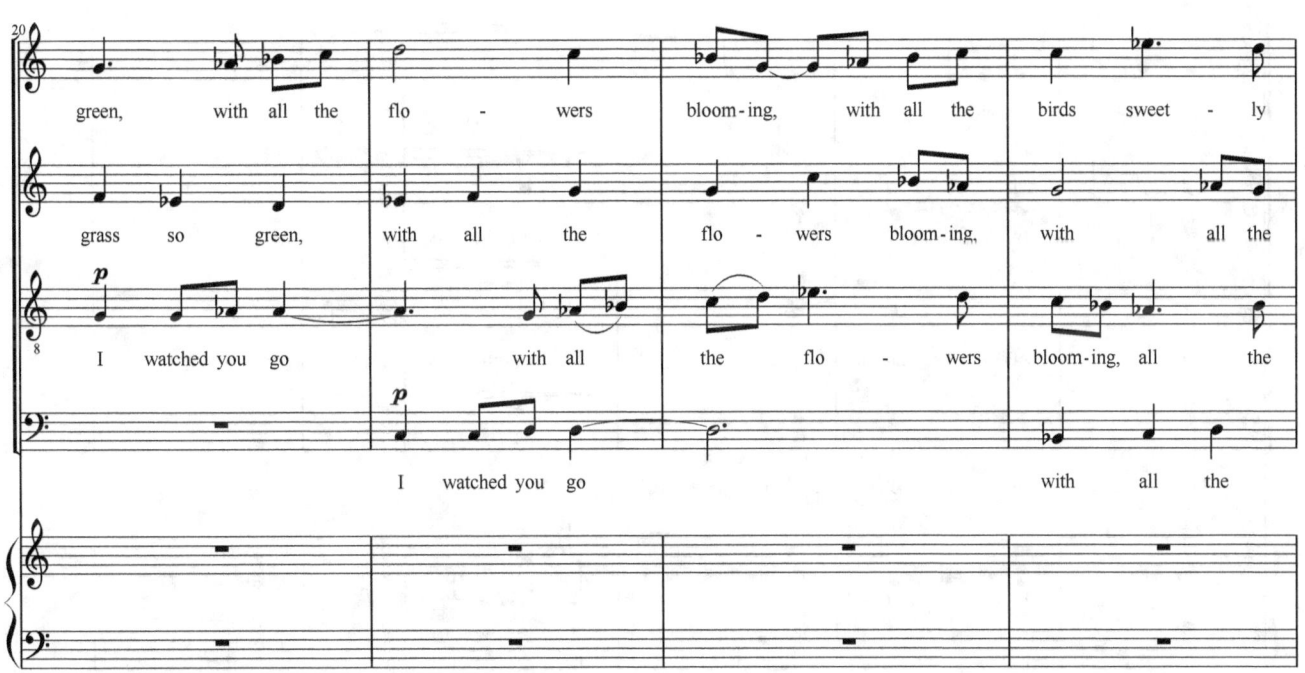

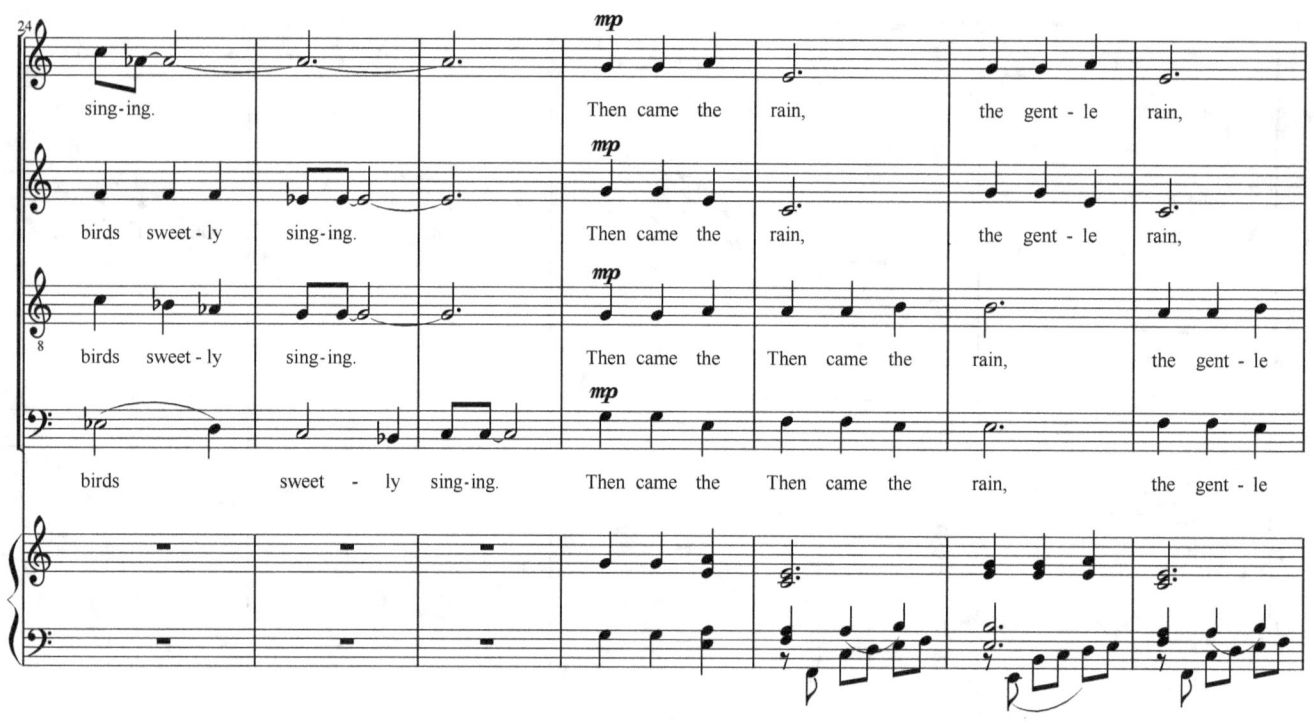

sing-ing. Then came the rain, the gent - le rain,

birds sweet - ly sing-ing. Then came the rain, the gent - le rain,

birds sweet - ly sing-ing. Then came the Then came the rain, the gent - le

birds sweet - ly sing-ing. Then came the Then came the rain, the gent - le

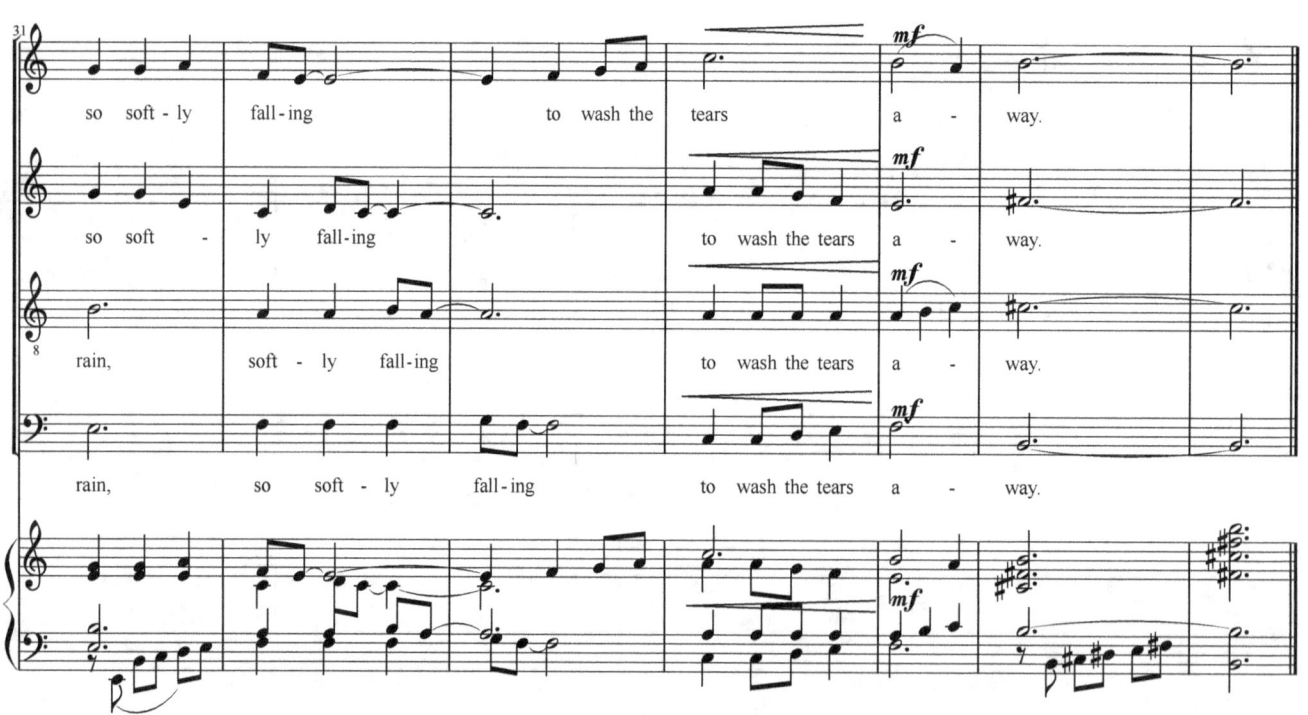

so soft-ly fall-ing to wash the tears a - way.

so soft - ly fall-ing to wash the tears a - way.

rain, soft - ly fall-ing to wash the tears a - way.

rain, so soft - ly fall-ing to wash the tears a - way.

Three Songs of Rain

Ken Langer

3. Dancing With the Rain

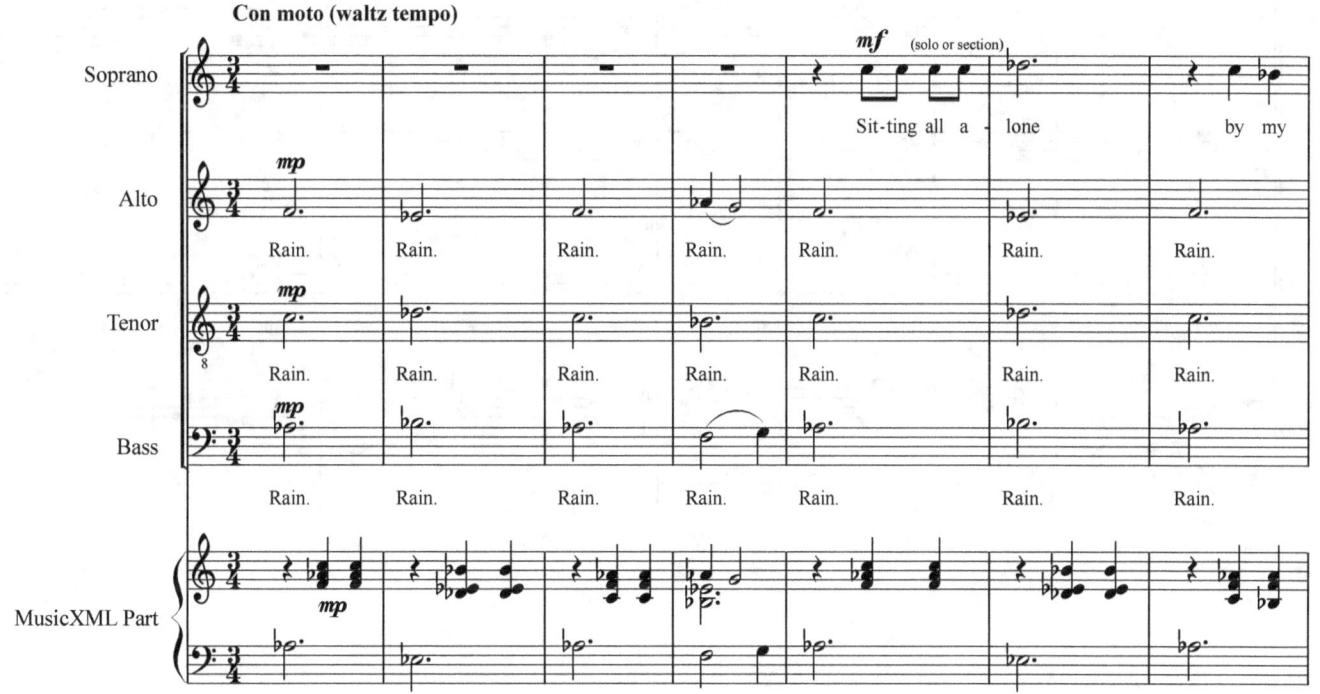

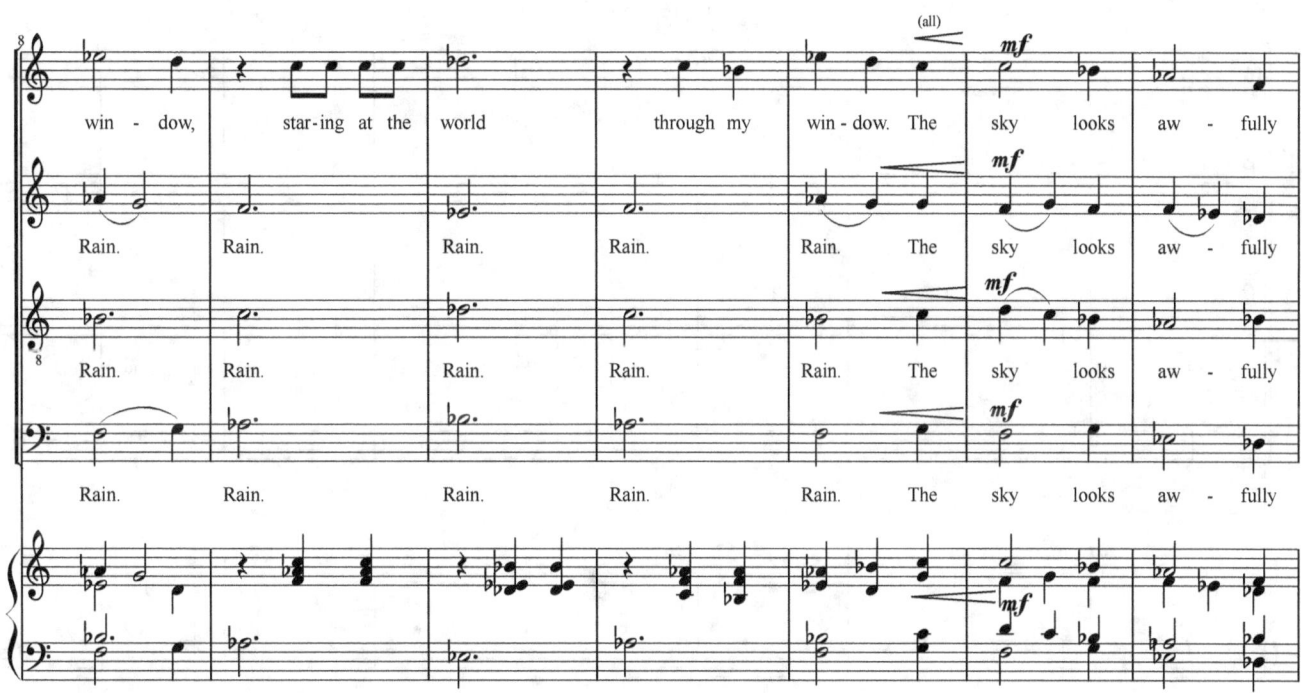

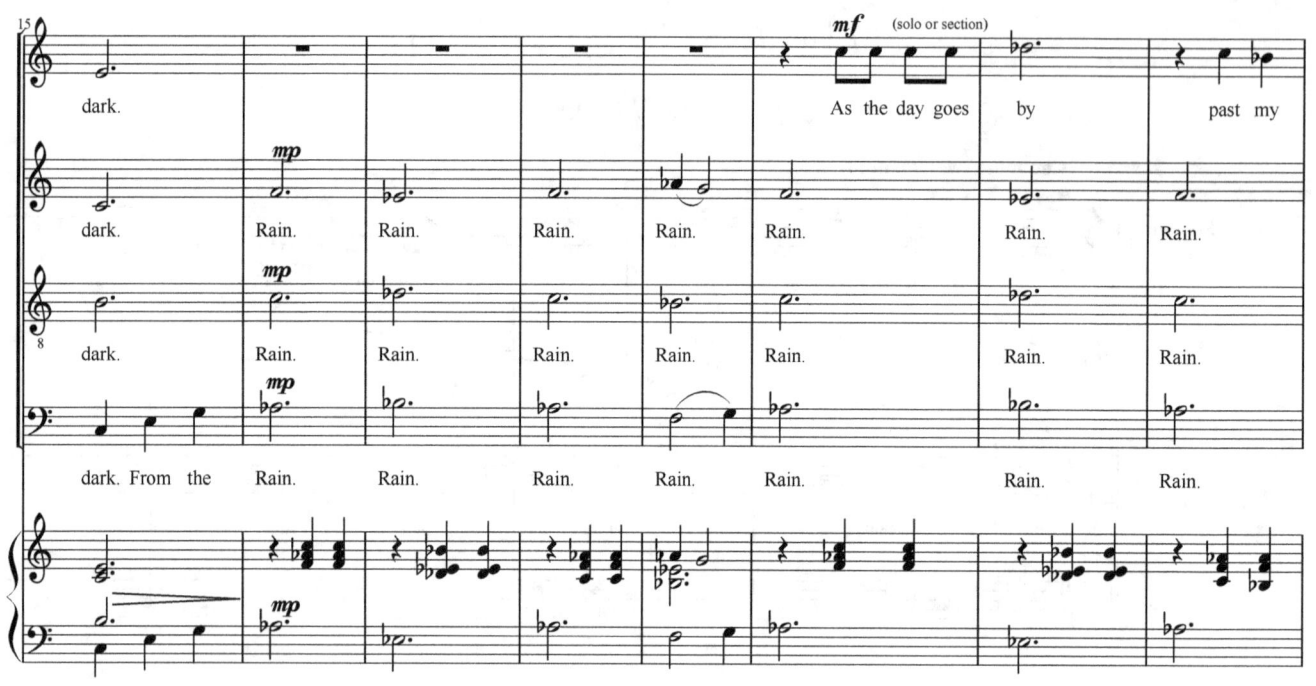

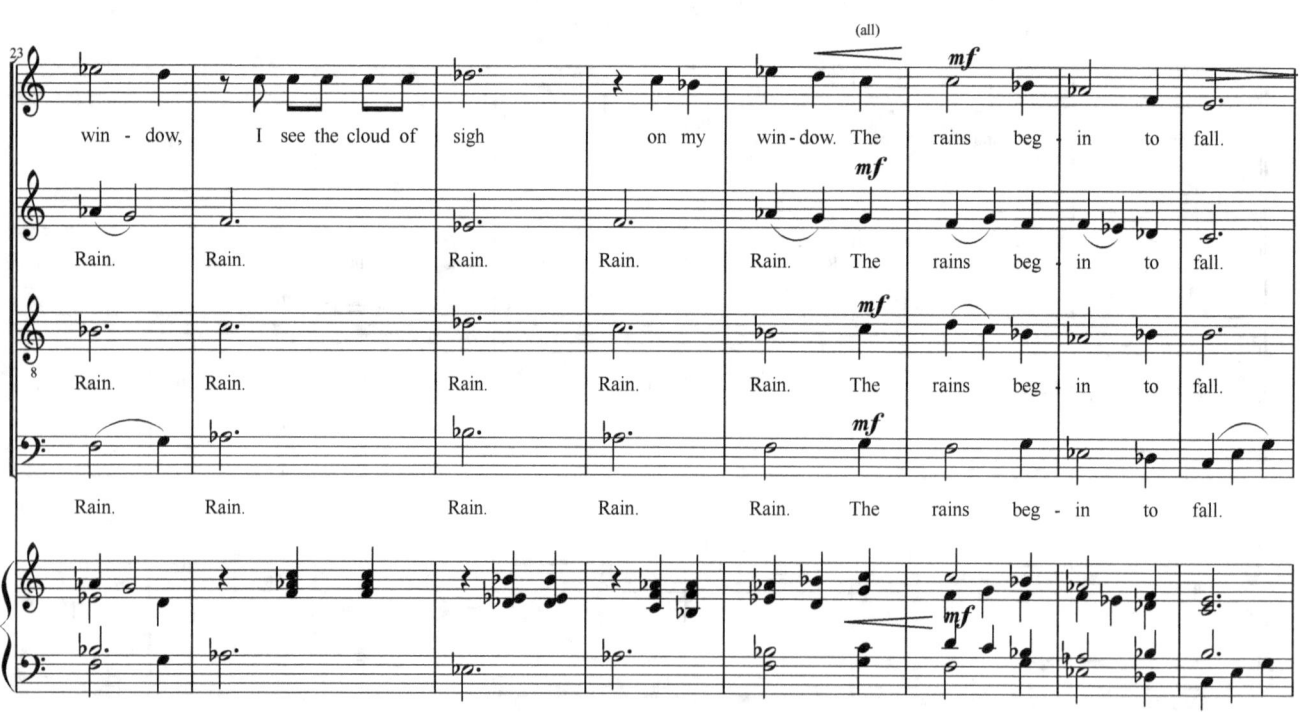

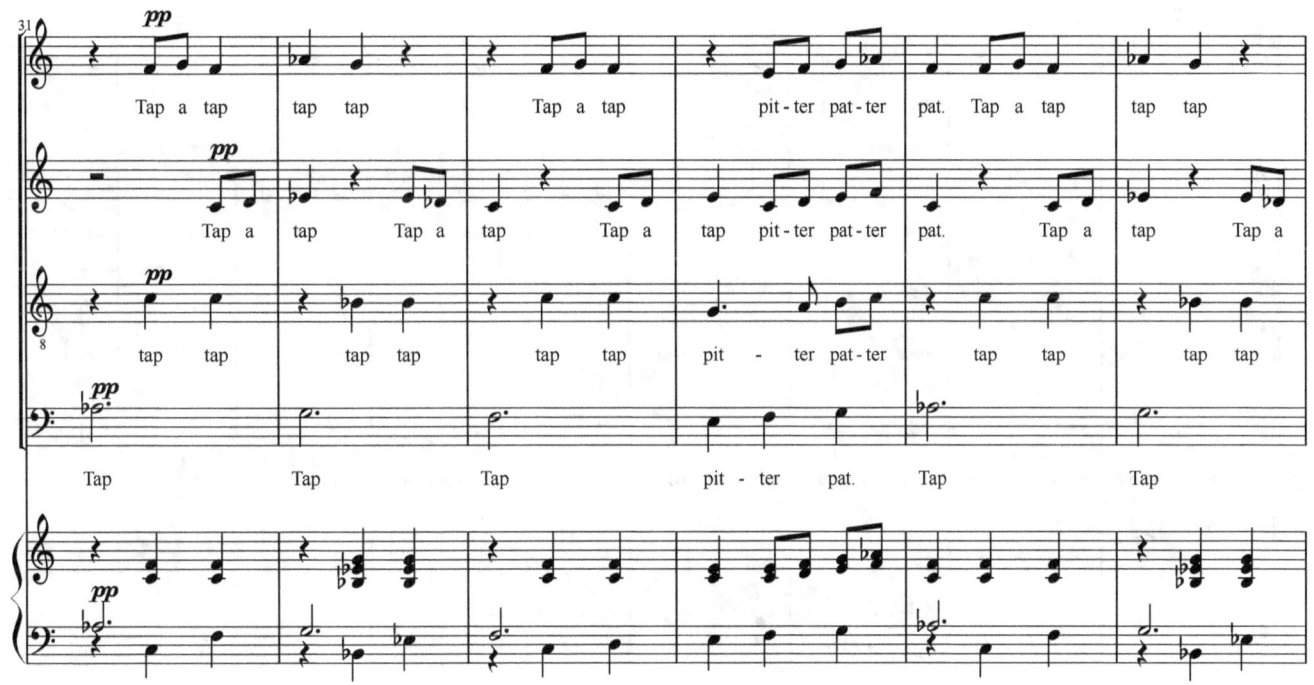

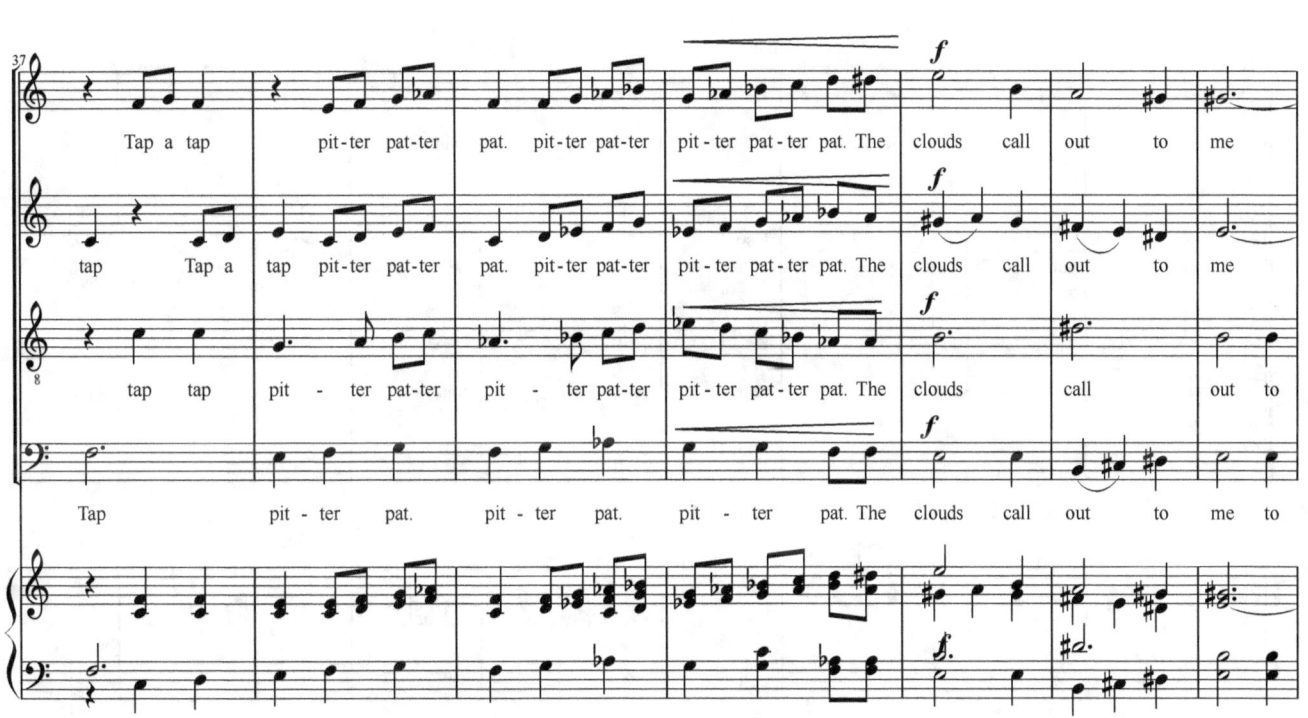

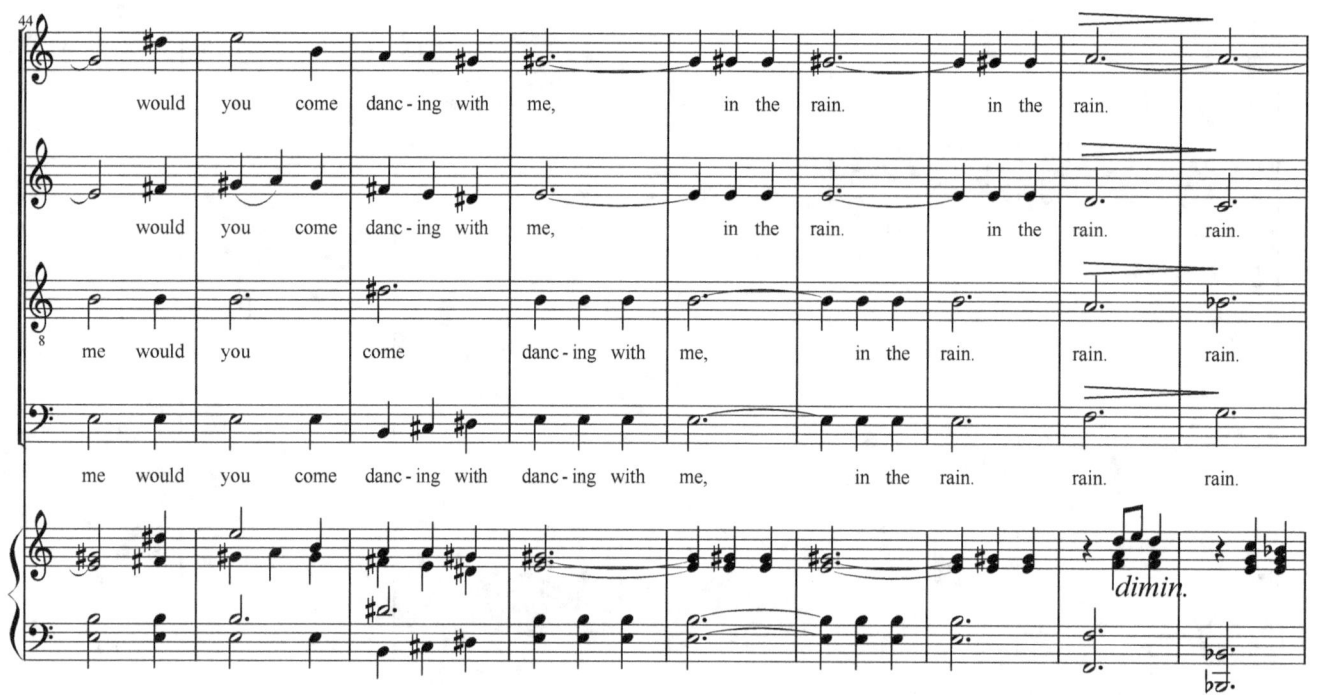

would you come danc-ing with me, in the rain. in the rain.

would you come danc-ing with me, in the rain. in the rain. rain.

me would you come danc-ing with me, in the rain. rain. rain.

me would you come danc-ing with danc-ing with me, in the rain. rain. rain.

dimin.

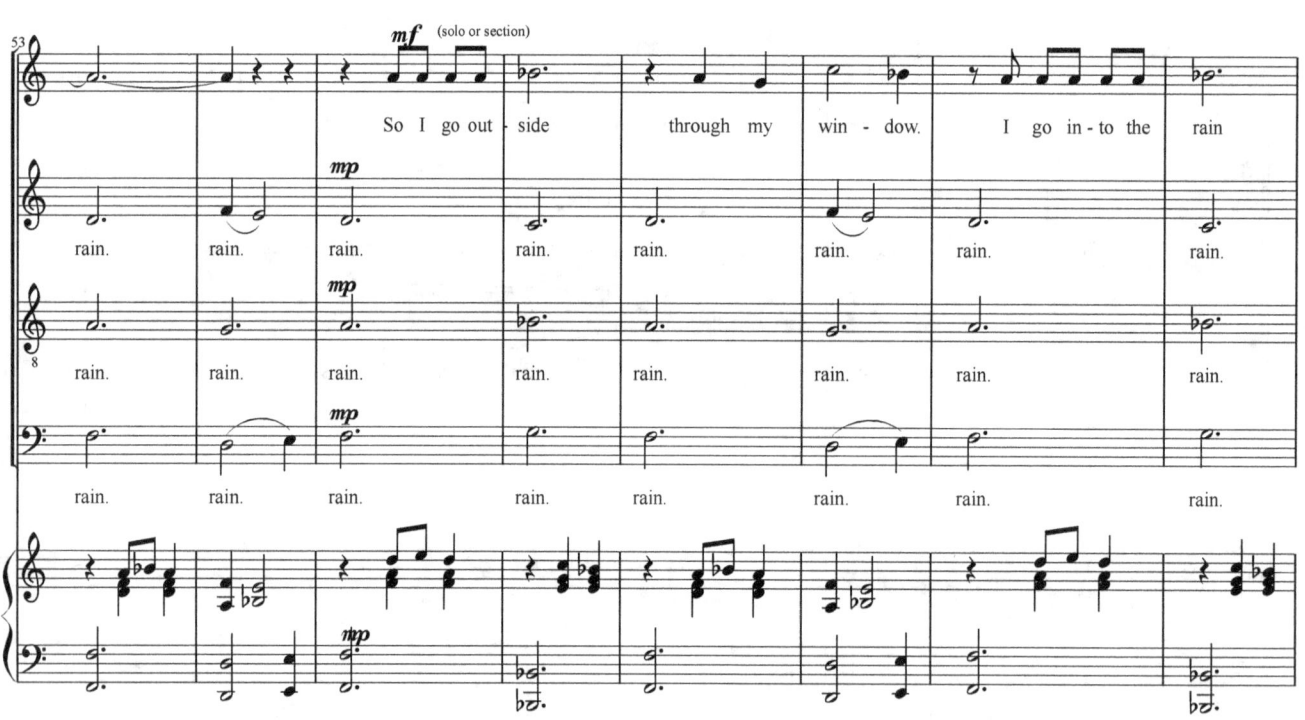

So I go out-side through my win-dow. I go in-to the rain

rain. rain. rain. rain. rain. rain. rain. rain.

rain. rain. rain. rain. rain. rain. rain. rain.

rain. rain. rain. rain. rain. rain. rain. rain.

mf (solo or section)

mp

mp

mp

mp

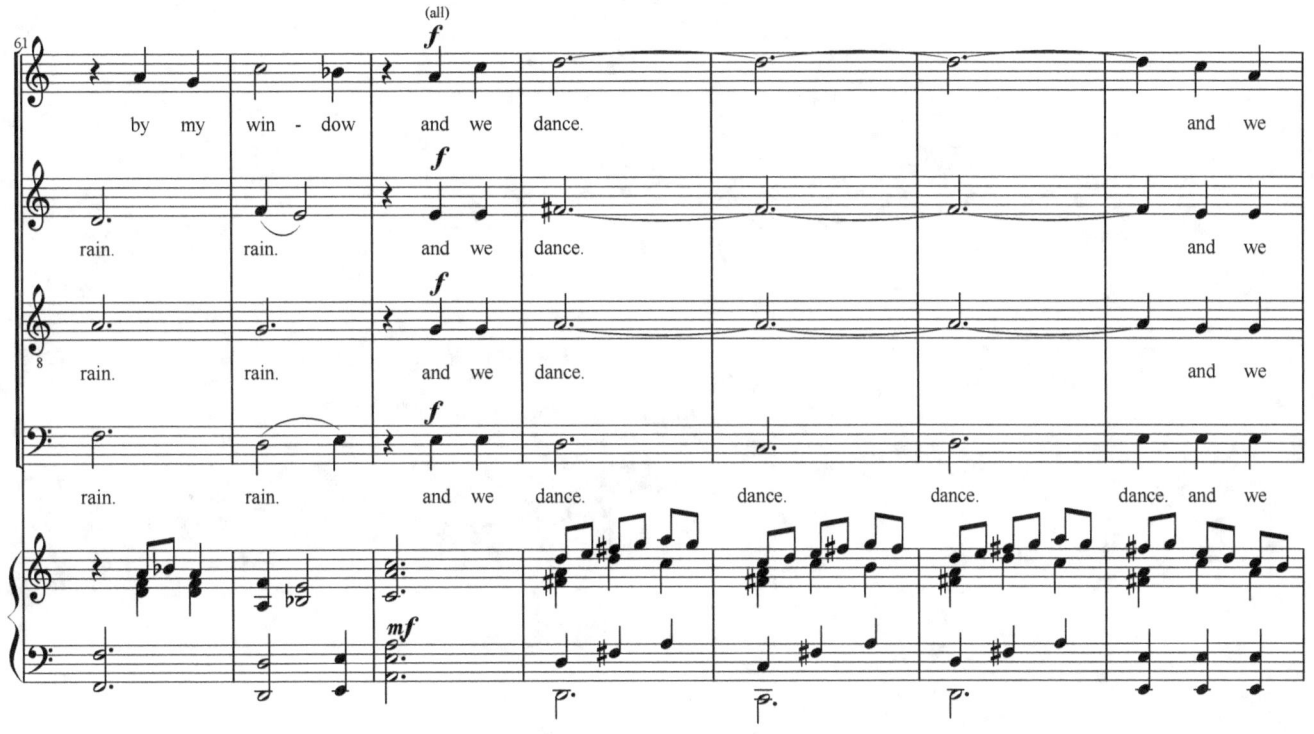

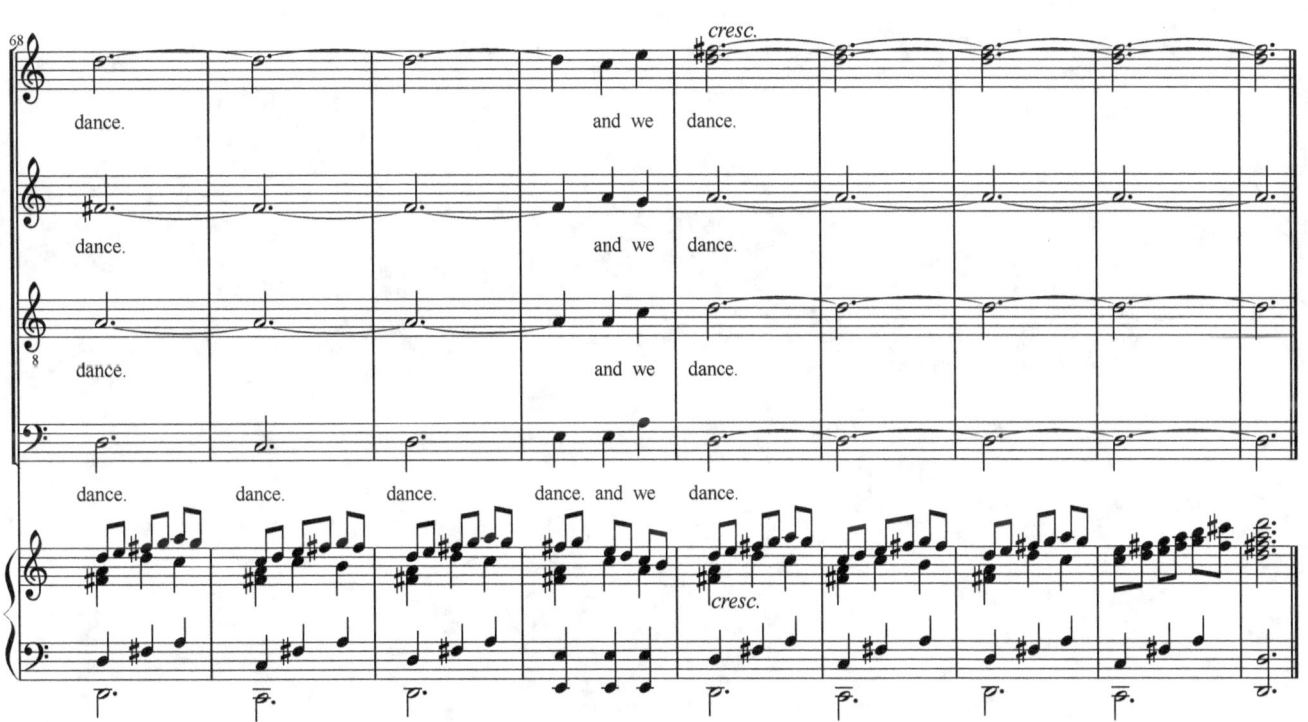

About The Composer

Dr. Kenneth Langer was born in the Pittsburgh area in 1959. He began playing trumpet in the 5th grade and decided in high school to make music his career.

Dr. Langer earned a Bachelor's Degree in Music Education at James Madison University in Harrisonburg, Virginia; a Master's of Music Degree at Radford University in Radford, Virginia; and a Ph.D. In Music Theory and Composition at Kent State University in Kent, Ohio. Since that time, he has taught music at several small colleges.

He has also been the full-time Director of Music and Arts at the Eno River Unitarian-Universalist Fellowship in Durham, North Carolina and the Assistant Conductor and Resident Composer at the Montpelier Unitarian-Universalist Church in Montpelier, Vermont.

During his twenty years of writing over 150 original works of music for various genres including brass, chorus, strings, orchestra, wind ensemble, and woodwinds; he has received numerous awards for his compositions including being named Vermont's Composer of the Year in the year 2000 and winning placement in several international composition contests. He has commercially published well over 30 compositions.

Dr. Langer currently lives in the Boston area with his family where he works as the Head of the Music Program at Northern Essex Community College in Haverhill, Massachusetts.

Publishers

Music For Brass

Nichols Music Company (Ensemble Publications)
P.O. Box 32 Ithaca, NY 14851-0032
www.enspub.com

Solid Brass Music
P.O. Box 2277 Rome GA, 30164
www.solidbrassmusic.com

Cimarron Music Press
15 Corrina Lane Salem CT 06420s
www.cimarronmusic.com

Wehr's Music House
www.wehrs-music-house.com

Music For Chorus

Yelton Rhodes Music
1236 N. Sweetzer Avenue #5 West Hollywood CA 90069
www.yrmusic.com

www.ingramcontent.com/pod-product-compliance
Lightning Source LLC
Chambersburg PA
CBHW081240180526
45171CB00005B/490